# Her Immaculate Hand

Selected Works By and About
The Women Humanists
of Quattrocento Italy

PEGASUS
PRESS

# Her Immaculate Hand

Selected Works By and About
The Women Humanists
of Quattrocento Italy

EDITED BY

## Margaret L. King

AND

## ALBERT RABIL, JR.

Pegasus Press
UNIVERSITY OF NORTH CAROLINA AT ASHEVILLE
ASHEVILLE, NORTH CAROLINA

Published by MRTS © 1983
Second edition revised © 1992
Reprinted 1997

© Copyright transferred 1997 to
*Pegasus Press*
ASHEVILLE, NORTH CAROLINA

**Library of Congress Cataloging-in-Publication Data**

Her immaculate hand : selected works by and about the women humanists of
Quattrocento Italy / edited by Margaret L. King and Albert Rabil, Jr.
p. cm.
Translations from Latin.
Includes bibliographical references (p. ) and index.
ISBN 0–86698–124–1 (paperbound)
  1. Latin literature, Medieval and modern—Women authors—Translations into
English.  2. Latin literature, Medieval and modern—Italy—Translations into
English.  3. Authors, Latin (Medieval and modern)—Italy—Correspondence.
4. Women—Italy—History—Renaissance, 1450–1600—Sources.  5. Italy—
Civilization—1266–1559—Sources. 6. Renaissance—Italy—Sources. 7. Human-
ists—Italy. I. King, Margaret L., 1947– . II. Rabil, Albert.
[PA8163.H47 1992]
305.4′0945′09024—dc20                                     92–22550
                                                              CIP

Printed in the United States of America

*To my daughter Alison*
*with much love,*
*and a heritage into which to enter*

*To my Mother*
*with much love,*
*a heritage embodied*

# Contents

## Part I: Women in the Public Arena

## Part II: Women on Women and Learning

## Part III: Men to Women

# *Preface*

The works of the women represented in this volume have never been translated from the Latin in which they wrote into any modern language. What is presented here is, in some cases, most of what is known to survive and, in others, only a small representation of a much larger production. Selections have been confined to women who lived during the Quattrocento, wrote in Latin, and regarded themselves—or desired to regard themselves—as part of the humanist movement so characteristic of the intellectual life of fifteenth–century Italy. Choice of the selections was determined both by their intrinsic interest and by their illumination of the problem women faced in entering the male world of humanist learning. Because we have focused on this problem, we have also chosen to include letters from male humanists to learned women in which they act as guides or counselors, giving advice of various kinds.

The translations have attempted to preserve the style of the Latin originals but at the same time to reflect contemporary idiomatic English, in some cases no easy task. We have been immensely aided by Professor Warren S. Smith of the Department of Classics, University of New Mexico, who has read our translations and saved us from many errors. For those that remain we accept full responsibility.

All the texts from which we worked are published but, with three exceptions, not in critical editions. We are, therefore, responsible also for references to various sources referred to by our authors.

The work has been a collaborative effort throughout. Each of us has worked on all the translations and introductions, as well as on the notes and bibliography. It is gratifying to bring to light sources which have lain hidden for so long. We hope students of the Renaissance and of women's history will find the effort well spent.

*January 1981*

MARGARET L. KING
DOUGLASTON, NEW YORK

ALBERT RABIL, JR.
WESTBURY, NEW YORK

## *Preface to the Second Edition*

The texts have remained basically unaltered in this new edition, except for two changes in note numbers. A Corrigenda has been added for errors in the text. There have been extensive changes in the notes, and we have updated the Bibliography. We are grateful to Professor Benjamin Kohl for many helpful suggestions in our revisions of the notes.

We are pleased that those interested in the intellectual lives of women in early modern Europe have continued to find this volume useful. We hope that an updated paperback edition will continue to keep it both useful and affordable for students at all levels.

September 1991

# *Corrigenda*

page 24, line 13  for critized *read* criticized
page 39, line 10  heir to *read* only child of
page 57, line 13  aked *read* asked
page 76, line 6  innumberable *read* innumerable
page 121, line 34  every sex *read* both sexes

# Introduction[1]

At the foot of a manuscript of Justinus that the young Ginevra Nogarola had copied, she proudly wrote: "I, Ginevra Nogarola, wrote this with my immaculate hand."[2] She was one of a new type the Italian Renaissance bequeathed to the modern world: the learned woman.

The learned woman appeared, in fact, at the same time as the men who espoused "the new learning." But her reception into that world by the men who reigned over it was complex. This complexity is reflected in two texts by learned men written near the beginning of the century, the first in honor of a learned woman, the second advising one.

The first is a poem and expository letter written by Antonio Loschi to Maddalena Scrovegni.[3] It was written in 1389, during the generation, that is, subsequent to the death of Petrarch (1304–74) when humanism established itself as a movement in Italy. Loschi's poem, entitled "The Temple of Chastity," and his expository letter explaining its symbolism are the earliest statements defining the figure of the learned woman during the Italian Renaissance. Loschi had already made Scrovegni's acquaintance prior to these works in her honor. After Scrovegni wrote to Jacopo dal Verme following the Visconti conquest of Padua in December 1388 (see the introduction to selection 1), Loschi, who had befriended the Visconti, was employed to respond to her on their behalf. He did so. In May of the following year, this time on his own behalf, he wrote to her a poem with an accompanying prose exposition. These were therefore addresses of one humanist to another and not politically inspired statements. In fact, Loschi in this second letter dissociates himself from his earlier one, asserting that "nothing but the style was my own, and not even that." In this letter he is his own master. He says he has decided to address her in poetry and to build her a "Temple of Chastity," for she had, in his view, so cultivated the virtue of chastity that she had become the incarnation of chastity itself. The Temple he will build is modelled on the little study in her father's house, the sight of which, as he says, first gave birth to the meditation he is now undertaking. The learned Maddalena seated in her study is thus transformed by Loschi's poetic imagination into the analogous figure of Chastity seated in her Temple.

The substance of the poem is as follows. In Scythia, the homeland of the warlike Amazons, there rises from an immense plain circled by the sea a lofty and wooded mountain. At its summit, visible from earth and sea, white marble walls enclose a courtyard filled with laurel and resounding with the cries of turtle doves. From there to the valley rushes a clear stream, where the goddess Diana, fatigued by the hunt, stops to drink. In the center of the courtyard stands the Temple of Chastity, within which burns the sacred flame of Vesta. Images of men and women famed for their chastity are incised on the marble of the interior walls: Hippolytus, Penelope, Dido, Lucretia and others. On a glass throne appears Chastity herself, mature of visage and weighty with dignity. At her feet sit the youthful twins Purity and Modesty. Surrounding this central group, each in a different posture, are the attendant figures of Continence, Penitence, and Virginity. The Temple is guarded by the formidable gatekeeper Frugality. When Cupid, armed with his mother's arrows, assails the hated Temple, he is repulsed sternly by Frugality and flees weeping. Repeatedly he attacks and is rebuffed, and abandons the battle exhausted, leaving Chastity intact.

In his expository letter Loschi explains the imagery. The frozen harshness of Scythia is conducive to the cultivation of chastity. The plain surrounded by the sea is our world engulfed by the bitterness of vice. The mountain rising above the plain is virtue focused on higher things. Thick forests suggest the difficulty of the ascent to the summit of virtue, concretized in the Temple sheltered behind shining white walls. Laurel trees, symbols of triumphant virtue, are planted in the courtyard and host the turtle doves famed for their chastity. The rushing stream cools the desires of the pure Diana when she seeks refuge from the hunt in which temptations assail her. Within the Temple, the Vestal flame represents the fiery heat of virtue residing in the soul and recalls the Roman virgins whose lives were dedicated to chastity. The interior of the Temple is adorned with the figures of those famed for heroic chastity (like the memory which stores the treasures of the mind). Chastity sits on a glass throne, because nothing is clearer or purer than glass, nor so easily violated. Her face is that of a mature widow, because true chastity has withstood many temptations. The twins Purity and Modesty are male (*Pudor*) and female (*Verecundia*) manifestations of the virtue of shame, appropriate to the young, who from their position at the feet of Chastity hold her model always before them. Continence stands close to Chastity, which cannot exist without her. Further away is Penitence, an older woman, who weeps for past sins. Still more remote is Virginity, young, timid and fearful, of undetermined character. Frugality guards the Temple gates because unrestrained indulgence in food and drink is a stimulus to desire—it was during a banquet that Cupid, sent by Venus, seduced Dido to her fateful love of Aeneas. But in the Temple of Chastity, Frugality prohibits such indulgence, and Cupid's repeated and clumsy attacks are repelled. Cupid's arrows powerless, Venus' armies and fortresses destroyed, Chastity triumphs.

There are two sets of interwoven associations in Loschi's poem and letter: chastity and power on the one hand, chastity and intelligence on the other. He identifies chastity with military strength at several points: in placing the Temple of Chastity in the land of the Amazons, in introducing the goddess Diana, in the figures of Chastity and Frugality themselves, in Cupid's assault on the Temple. The image of the Amazons is most important. The warlike Amazons are chaste (uncorrupted) and the climate of their rule frigid, more suited to chastity than to the soft warmth of Italy. The military associations are masculine. Diana, Chastity and Frugality, all are more masculine than feminine in character. Only Virginity, in her vulnerability, appears to be feminine. Chastity survives because she is stronger than lust. Where Venus is soft, Chastity is aggressive, bellicose, virile.

Chastity is associated with intelligence as well as with power. Maddalena's study, the site of her intellectual activity, is identified by the author with the Temple that houses the personification of Chastity. That same Temple is later identified with memory, a major function of mind, and the images engraved on its walls are identified with thoughts stored in memory. The Temple of Chastity appears to be the mind of Maddalena, in which she is ensconced like a strong but captive goddess. By these strange links, Maddalena's learning is bound to the chastity by which she wins the regard of the poet.

The question arises: Why did Loschi choose to memorialize Scrovegni's chastity, in which she was merely conforming to a conventional standard of behavior, rather than her learning, in which she was unique? His emphasis was not peculiar to him but reappears again and again, for example, in eulogies of Isotta Nogarola, Cassandra Fedele, and Costanza Varano (see selections 20 and 24). The imagery expresses the respect that male humanists feel toward learned women, but also the fear, and in response to that fear, the desire to restrain them by exceptionally rigid demands of chastity. Intellectual women are perceived as fierce. Because they are fierce, they are required to be chaste. In welding together the triadic qualities of intellect, strength and chastity, Loschi transmits and affirms an enduring literary tradition which defines implacably the role of the learned woman. He erects for Scrovegni a temple in her honor and binds her captive within it.

The second text revealing the complex attitude of male humanists towards learned women is a letter written in 1405 by Leonardo Bruni (1369–1444) to Battista da Montefeltro Malatesta.[4] In it he outlined the new learning as it should apply to women. The new learning, Bruni writes, has nothing to do "with that vulgar threadbare jargon which satisfies those who devote themselves to Theology," but with classical Latin. The foundations of this new learning, therefore, rest upon a "sound and thorough knowledge of Latin: which implies study marked by a broad spirit, accurate scholarship, and careful attention to details." Without this "the great monuments of literature are unintelligible, and the art of composition impossible."[5] The monuments of literature are, among Christian writers, the Latin theologians Augustine, Jerome, Ambrose, Cyprian, and Lactantius; the Greek theologians (in Latin translation) Gregory of Nazianzen, Chrysostom, and Basil; and the classical pagan (Latin) writers Cicero, Virgil, Livy, Sallust. Careful attention to these writers will make one stylistically a good Latinist.

As to subject matter, Bruni says Battista should avoid the subtleties of arithmetic, geometry, and astrology, none of which is worthy of a cultivated mind. Women, in particular, should also avoid rhetoric. The latter has no practical value for her since she does not engage in public debate.[6] Later, however, Bruni suggests that she study the great orators in order to learn, in her *writing*, how to express consolation, encouragement, dissuasion or advice, as well as to learn eloquent expression, a large vocabulary, and a free-flowing style.[7] It appears, then, that a woman should study oratory, but with a view to improving her writing skills rather than her public speaking skills, since the latter, in his view, would be inappropriate.

As to other disciplines, she should give her attention first and foremost to religion and morals. For this purpose she need not confine herself to Christian writers but may gain a great deal as well from pagan writers who have written much about continence, temperance, modesty, justice, courage, and greatness of soul. History is also commendable, because it gives us knowledge of our origins as well as a store of moral examples by which to live and with which to adorn our writings. Somewhat condescendingly he adds: "Such writers are fully within the comprehension of a studious lady. For, after all, history is an easy subject: there is nothing in its study subtle or complex. It consists in the narration of the simplest matters of fact which, once grasped, are readily retained in the memory."[8]

Finally, he recommends the poets. Every educated woman must be thoroughly familiar with them, "for we cannot point to any great mind of the past for whom the poets had not a powerful attraction."[9] Aristotle quotes Homer, Hesiod, Pindar, Euripides, and other poets. Even the Church fathers abound in poetic allusions. Moreover, the poets express everything with exquisite grace and dignity. Bruni alludes to those who reject the study of the poets. Boccaccio had had to defend poetry during the preceding century, and just a short time before Bruni penned his letter to Battista, Giovanni Dominici, a Florentine cleric, had publicly opposed the study of pagan poetry, calling forth a rejoinder from Coluccio Salutati, humanist chancellor of the city of Florence and a spiritual father to Bruni. Poetry, Bruni says, has a peculiar affinity to our emotions and intelligence, and moves us as nothing else can do. If there are some stories of pagan poets that equate love and sin, we should remember that they are fictions and are to be read allegorically rather than literally and, furthermore, that there are many stories of a different kind in them. A woman should not read the vulgar, second-rate poets, but she should certainly read the best ones.

Nearly the entire program of the new learning has here been commended to a woman. It consists of the disciplines of grammar, rhetoric, history, poetry and moral philosophy. These, indeed, were the province of the humanists, and in the sense described by Bruni. Grammar builds a precise and detailed knowledge of classical Latin; rhetoric embellishes that Latin both in terms of subjects to be discussed and expressions to be employed; history teaches us our origins, provides moral examples for living and gives us illustrations for writing; poetry moves and awakens in us the most exalted feelings; moral philosophy teaches us the virtues by which we are to live.

With one exception Bruni commends the same education to women as to men. The exception, however, is significant. Bruni did not envision women in the public arena. It was not decorous, he believed, to see women speaking in public or taking on public functions. Study was perfectly appropriate to women, but not the public display of their learning. The tension that such an attitude might cause—and in this case did cause—is not difficult to see. Women are encouraged to become highly cultured, and in a way characteristic of men who, by virtue of that culture, become public figures; but they are denied the public arena for which these disciplines prepare them. That denial leads to difficulties for the learned women of the fifteenth century which are evident in their lives and works. In addition to excepting rhetoric as an appropriate object of study, Bruni also makes one other qualification: the education of women is to focus more heavily upon religion than that of men. This recommendation, echoed by other male humanists, as will be amply evident in the texts translated here, is related as well to attitudes that confined women to the private arena.

The program of study Bruni outlines finds a resonance in the lives of the learned women of the century. Most of them paid close attention to religion. At the same time, however, they wrote poetry, letters, orations, moral philosophy, biography and autobiography. They employed on occasion the dialogue form characteristic of many humanist treatises on moral philosophy. They even shared in that genre of writing created by the humanists: invective. They did not, it seems, write histories, and for good reason: they were unable to sustain public careers as humanists, which otherwise involved commissions from cities or rulers, access to public records, and the extended time to write which this genre required.[10] For the same reason, they did not write letters as public officials, secretaries, or diplomats. But they did, contrary to Bruni's advice, appear in public on a number of occasions. These appearances, however, did not help them build public careers for themselves as humanists. On the contrary, they served to sharpen the tensions implicit in both Loschi and Bruni.

## Who Were the Women Humanists?

Quattrocento Italy produced a number of learned women who participated in humanism, the characteristic intellectual movement of the Renaissance. Some rose above obscurity because they left works of their own or because they were addressed as learned women by others. Ten of them are represented in this anthology. There are perhaps twenty more who are known to us by name, but about whom little information is available. The group we know is sufficiently large to suggest that humanist culture touched many more women than we know as it spread across Northern Italy.[11]

The earliest of the women humanists considered here was Maddalena Scrovegni (1356–1429), born into a noble Paduan family.[12] She was married in 1376 to a nobleman of Reggio but widowed shortly thereafter, and by 1381 she had reestablished her home in Padua. In 1390 she fled the city with her family when the Visconti forces of Milan (which her family supported) lost the city to the Carrara. She remained in Venice until her death in 1429. Maddalena was a learned woman, as attested by an extant letter of her own (selection 1) and by two learned men. Lombardo della Seta, humanist and companion of Petrarch, dedicated to her a work on famous women (now lost) in which he praised her learning; and Antonio Loschi (1365–1441) wrote the letter and poem in her honor analyzed earlier.

Battista da Montefeltro Malatesta (1383–1450) was the younger daughter of Antonio, Count of Urbino. Before her marriage in 1405 to Galeazzo Malatesta, heir to the lordship of Pesaro, she had cultivated a great interest in classical Latin antiquity, as suggested by the fact that Bruni addressed to her the letter on learning already discussed. Her marriage seems to have been unhappy from the beginning. Her husband, once he gained power, proved a perfidious ruler, and was assassinated after two years (1429–31). Thereafter until her death, she lived in her old home of Urbino, where she found in her father-in-law a man who shared her literary interests. The two of them exchanged *canzoni* and Latin letters, some of which are extant. When the Emperor Sigismund passed through Urbino in 1433 she greeted him with a Latin oration (selection 2). She was the mother of one daughter and the grandmother of one of the best known of learned women, Costanza Varano, whom she helped educate. She died as a Sister of the Franciscan Order of Saint Claire.[13]

The first generation of women humanists born during the Quattrocento includes six of some renown: Isotta Nogarola (1418–66), her sister Ginevra

Nogarola (1417–1461/8), Costanza Barbaro (b. after 1419), Cecilia Gonzaga (1425–51), Costanza Varano (1428–47), and Caterina Caldiera (d. 1463).

The first mentioned, Isotta Nogarola, is also perhaps the most famous and accomplished learned woman of the century.[14] She learned Latin and Greek at an early age, studying with Martino Rizzoni, a pupil of Guarino of Verona (1374–1460), one of the great humanist teachers of the Quattrocento. Through Rizzoni, perhaps, Isotta, as well as her sister Ginevra, became known to the circle around Guarino. At the age of eighteen Isotta entered into correspondence with a number of these humanists, hoping to enter their circle and engage in literary discourse. During the next two years she corresponded with Guarino's son, Girolamo, and with Giorgio Bevilacqua and Ludovico Cendrata, two of Guarino's disciples. Both sisters wrote to the son of the Venetian Doge, Giacomo Foscari, who showed their letters to Guarino. Guarino in a letter to Giacomo praised the two sisters, then reported on their talents to Leonello d'Este, son of the Duke of Ferrara, whose tutor Guarino was. At length Isotta wrote to Guarino himself, who did not respond. Isotta was made the laughing-stock of Verona, for it was public knowledge that she had written Guarino. Shaken by this turn of events, she wrote to Guarino again, explaining to him how his silence had made her an object of ridicule. This, finally, drew from Guarino a reply praising Isotta and encouraging her in her studies.

After two years, however, Isotta stopped writing. Why? The men with whom she corresponded praised her, but they praised her because she excelled other women in her learning, not because her learning equalled that of men. They also suggested that if Isotta would achieve her goals, she must cease to be a woman and become a man. This sentiment was more correct than perhaps the writers understood. For they were saying in effect that there was no place for a woman in the world of humanism.

As if this message were not clear enough, one anonymous writer in Verona, calling himself "Pliny," addressed a letter to his friend "Ovid" in 1438 in which he accused Isotta of incest with her brother and, most strikingly of all, linked this outrageous accusation with her learning, remarking that the saying "of many wise men I hold to be true: that an eloquent woman is never chaste; and the behavior of many learned women also confirms its truth."[15] It is not surprising that by 1438 Isotta had given up her ambition to become a humanist.

But the most striking thing about Isotta—what makes her unique among all the learned women of the century—is that she did not give up her ideal of devoting herself to the life of the mind. After three years of indecision during which she lived in Venice (1438–41), she returned to Verona, having decided neither to marry nor to accept religious vows, but to live in her own home (with her mother), devoting herself to sacred studies. This she did for twenty-five years. From 1453 we hear of bodily illness, perhaps associated with her

religious vigils, which may eventually have contributed to her death. The illness may well have been related to the fact that in order to maintain her intellectual life, Isotta had to pay a high price: perpetual chastity and isolation
from other learned people.

Her isolation was significantly broken for only one short period during these
years, 1451–53, when she entered into correspondence with Ludovico Foscarini,
a Venetian nobleman and humanist. In his letters he encourages her chastity
and, like Loschi before him, links learning with chastity. To insure the union,
he cherishes and commends to Isotta his image of her locked in her little cell
with Christ and urges her to remain there. When she received an unexpected
proposal of marriage at the age of thirty-five in 1453, she referred the matter
to Foscarini, who wrote back much agitated that she should think of giving
up the chastity to which she had bound herself. She accepted his advice.

The most significant of her writings comes out of this period of her intense
relationship to Foscarini: a dialogue on the respective responsibilities of Adam
and Eve for the fall (selection 10). Foscarini defended Adam, Nogarola Eve.
But her defense rests upon the denigration of her sex: Eve is weak and cannot
be held as responsible as Adam who is strong and perfect. Isotta paid a high
price indeed for her right to continue her studies. The wonder is that she continued at all.

Her sister Ginevra did not. As girls the two sisters were trained together
by the same tutor, and both were equally known, even addressed jointly by
some humanists. But in 1438, the year during which Isotta gave up her ambition of becoming a humanist, Ginevra married a Brescian nobleman, Brunoro
Gambara, and gave her life over to raising a large family and working within
the community. Her life as a humanist seems to have ended completely with
her marriage.

Two other learned women of this generation took the same step as Ginevra:
marriage. Costanza Varano (1426–47) was the granddaughter of Battista da
Montefeltro Malatesta.[16] Although born in Camerino, her mother fled with
the children to Pesaro in 1434 after Costanza's father had been slain by his
brothers. It was in Pesaro that she received her education, partly at the hands
of her grandmother, who was now devoted to the religious life. By the time
of her marriage to Alessandro Sforza, lord of Pesaro, on December 8, 1444,
she was an accomplished Latinist. Several of her letters, orations, and poems
are preserved, of which three are translated here (selections 4, 8, and 9). But
after her marriage her studies ceased. She gave birth to a daughter, Battista
(1446–72), later the second wife of Federico da Montefeltro (1422–82), and
to a son, Costanzo, eight days after whose birth she died.

Caterina Caldiera (d. 1463) was the daughter of the Venetian humanist and
physician, Giovanni Caldiera.[17] Her early studies focused on Latin authors

of classical antiquity. Her father composed for her a commentary on a school text attributed to one of the ancient Catos, designed to introduce his daughter not only to the virtues of temperance and diligence in study but also to various forms of philosophy and mythology. He later revised this work for her and says in his new preface that she had written a work *De laudibus sanctorum* (not known to be extant). He goes on to praise her learning and to claim that it is recognized by others as well as by him. In a second work addressed to her he again refers to her interest in sacred literature but counsels her not to abandon pagan myths inasmuch as they embody Christian truth in veiled form. In addition to her father, Filippo da Rimini praised her poetry and Antonio Vinciguerra her learning in general. In 1451, however, she married Andrea Contarini, after which she gave birth to several children and ran a patrician household, perhaps precluding the possibility of continuing her studies. Nothing of what she wrote before her marriage is extant. Less well-known in her accomplishments than others in this group, she nonetheless illustrates the diffusion of humanist culture. She illustrates also the importance of fathers in the education of their daughters. Caterina appears to have been trained by her father—no other teachers are mentioned. With exceptions to be noted, humanist schools were not generally open to girls. Many who became learned did so at home.

The last two women in this group, Costanza Barbaro and Cecilia Gonzaga, both entered the religious life. Costanza (b. after 1419) was the eldest and favorite daughter of the Venetian statesman and humanist, Francesco Barbaro (1390–1454).[18] Francesco studied under three well-known teachers of his time: Giovanni Conversini da Ravenna, Gasparino Barzizza, and Guarino da Verona. He learned Greek thoroughly and in 1415, still a young man, astonished humanist circles with a treatise *On Marriage*.[19] Shortly after this, he assumed a political career and married, continuing his humanist activities in a voluminous Latin correspondence and through patronage. Of his four daughters, at least Costanza was trained in humanist studies, perhaps alongside her brother Zuccaria. By June 1440, when Costanza was about twenty, she resolved to enter a convent. By 1448 she had been joined by her sister Ginevra, and before 1453 a third sister, Lucrezia, entered another convent. A fourth sister, Paola, married in 1453. There is some indication from a letter written to a friend that Francesco would have preferred that his eldest daughter remain in the world, though he did not oppose her wish to enter the religious life. The strongest evidence we have that she entered the religious life in part to continue her studies is her father's letter to her in 1447 consoling her on the death of her cousin, Luchina (selection 18). The letter is full of classical allusions and reveals a strong cultural bond between father and daughter.

Cecilia (1425–51) was the daughter of Gianfrancesco Gonzaga (1395–1444) and Paola Malatesta da Rimini.[20] Gianfrancesco was responsible for bringing to Mantua in 1423 the humanist teacher, Vittorino da Feltre (1378–1446), for the purpose of educating his growing family. Vittorino established a school away from the court which came to be known as "the house of joy," in which a program of classical studies — both Christian and pagan — was combined with physical activity. With Vittorino, Cecilia studied Greek and Latin and excelled in both. She is said to have achieved competence in Greek by the time she was eight years old. When she was eighteen (1443) she resolved to enter a convent. Her father opposed her wish, desiring that she marry Oddantonio di Montefeltro, who had succeeded to the Dukedom of Urbino in 1442. Oddantonio became so hated by his subjects that in 1444 he was murdered by them. Perhaps because of his growing reputation for evil, Cecilia's father apparently withdrew his demand that she marry Oddantonio, but he still did not wish her to enter a convent. Her pious mother, Paola, supported her intentions, as did Vittorino and a former student of Vittorino's, the humanist Gregorio Correr (see selection 17). None of this support proved effective, though Cecilia was freed from the conflict by the death of her father in 1444 and immediately took the veil. Her mother entered the convent with her. That Cecilia entered the religious life at least in part to continue her studies is strongly suggested by the letter of Gregorio Correr written to strengthen her resolve. In it she is encouraged to use her learning for religious ends.

The second generation of Quattrocento women humanists, those who flourished between 1460 and 1480, finds only one who stands out, Ippolita Sforza (1445–88), daughter of Francesco Sforza (1401–66) and Bianca Maria Visconti (1425–68).[21] Bianca Maria was the heir of Filippo Maria Visconti, her father and ruler of Milan; she married Francesco Sforza in 1441. Filippo Maria died in 1447, and the Milanese established the Ambrosian Republic. That, however, was short-lived, and Francesco established himself as Duke of Milan in 1450. No sooner had he secured his rule than he sought to win over his people by beautifying the city and making it a center of culture. Machiavelli says of him in *The Prince* that "Francesco by the proper means and through his own ability rose from private station to be Duke of Milan and preserved with little effort the duchy which had cost him many pains to acquire."[22] Pope Pius II (Enea Silvio Piccolomini, a leading humanist before he became pope in 1458) met him at Mantua in 1459, on which occasion Ippolita addressed the pontiff (selection 6). Pius wrote of him in his *Commentaries* that he married a lady of great beauty and virtue by whom he had a number of handsome children. Among his children were Ludovico Il Moro, the favorite of his mother Bianca Maria, and later ruler of Milan; Ascanio Maria, who later became a cardinal and to whom, as cardinal, Laura Cereta dedicated her published letters; and Ippolita.

In the vibrant cultural atmosphere of the new Sforza dynasty in Milan, Ippolita received, together with her numerous brothers and sisters (legitimate and illegitimate) a true humanist education. She studied Greek with the Greek Costantino Lascaris, and Latin with two scholars: Guiniforte Barzizza, son of the famous founder of the school of humanist studies in Milan, Gasparino Barzizza, and with Baldo Martorello, a pupil of Vittorino's. She was betrothed when she was only ten to Alfonso, Duke of Calabria, whom she married in 1465. Prior to her marriage she composed works in the Latin humanist tradition, two of which are extant and included in this anthology (selections 5 and 6). After her marriage we have nothing from her pen. However, as Duchess of Calabria she became a friend and patron of men of letters and collected a rich library in the Castel Capuano in Naples where she lived. Several humanist works were dedicated to her. In this respect she resembles Battista Sforza, the daughter of Costanza Varano, already discussed, Isabella d'Este (1474–1539), the Marchioness of Mantua, and Elizabetta Gonzaga (1471–1526), the Duchess of Urbino (immortalized in Castiglione's *Courtier*), that is, a learned woman more noted as a political figure, whose education contributed to her political and social competence and who encouraged a high culture through her patronage, rather than as a writer who contributed to it through her own productions.[23]

The third generation of Quattrocento women humanists, those who flourished between 1480 and 1500, includes several prominent figures: Cassandra Fedele (1465–1558), Laura Cereta (1469–99) and Alessandra Scala (1475–1506).

Cassandra Fedele belonged to the privileged *cittadino* class in Venice, and her relatives often worked in the bureaucracies of the state, so that she was in a position to be noticed.[24] Her family had a long tradition of learning, her father, grandfather and great-grandfather all having achieved some repute. Her father was notable for his humanist training, and his humanist endeavors were supported by Venetian patrons of letters. He had her tutored in Latin and Greek by the theologian and humanist Gasparino Borro, permitting these studies priority over her domestic activities. She had mastered Latin by the age of twelve, and subsequently studied Greek, rhetoric, history, some elements of philosophy, and sacred letters. The culmination of these studies were public appearances in which she delivered orations before the University of Padua (selection 11), the people of Venice (selection 7) and the Venetian Doge Agostino Barbarigo. She won the favor of the latter, who invited her to receptions attended by Venetian writers, poets, and prominent citizens. In 1488, when she was twenty-two, Queen Isabella of Spain invited Cassandra to her court, but she was prohibited from going by the Venetian Senate on the grounds that Venice could not spare such an asset to the state. She was now at the height of her fame and powers. In 1491 the Florentine poet and humanist, Angelo Poliziano, wrote her one of the most glowing letters of praise received by any woman from a male humanist during the century (selection 23).

Her intellectual attainments to this point in her life reflect competence but no originality of mind. Her orations are fairly conventional statements of humanist wisdom. She had, however, established a basis of learning on which she might have built. But this was not to happen. Apparently those who encouraged her early achievement never intended that she pursue her studies further. She was an intellectual asset to Venice in 1488, not as a person learned beyond others of her age, but as a prodigy, unusual because she was a learned *woman*. When, with advancing age, she could no longer be regarded as a prodigy, the only alternative was to marry her off, and this was done, to Giammaria Mappelli, a physician of Vicenza, around 1497.

From the time of her marriage Cassandra suffered a chronic illness, perhaps psychosomatic (as one might conjecture in the case of Isotta Nogarola as well). This may well have been related to her being forced to accept a conventional social role with which she was not entirely happy. Unlike other women discussed thus far who married, however, Cassandra had no children (perhaps this also was connected with her chronic illness). Unlike them also, she returned to her literary pursuits while still married, though only after a hiatus of seventeen years (selection 24). Seven years later still her husband died, and Cassandra returned to Venice (1521) where she lived the remainder of her long life—she died in 1558 at the age of ninety-three. Despite the length of her life, however, and her eventual freedom from both marriage and children, she never resumed her humanistic studies to the extent that her early productivity might have suggested.

On the contrary, what we have from her pen in these later years are two letters, the primary purpose of which is to find relief from the straitened economic circumstances in which her husband's death had left her. The first of these letters, addressed to Pope Leo X in 1521, shortly after her husband had died, requests assistance, but without effect. The pope never replied or intervened in her behalf. Twenty-six years later, when she was eighty-two, she wrote to Pope Paul III expressing an even greater distress. In this case the pope intervened with the Venetian Senate to have her appointed prioress of the orphanage attached to the Church of San Domenico di Castello. The Senate concurred, and she held this position until her death in 1558. It is both remarkable and sad that the city she had honored as a young woman ignored her when she was old and in need of its assistance until importuned from outside. Having been prodded into helping her, however, the city fathers also made one more use of her talent. In 1556, at the age of ninety-one, she delivered an oration welcoming to Venice the Queen of Poland (selection 7).

In some respects the life of Laura Cereta parallels that of Cassandra Fedele, except that it is telescoped into one-third the life span.[25] Laura was born the eldest of six children; two sisters and three brothers followed. She always felt most loved, and attributed this to the fact that she was the oldest child. When she was seven she was sent to a convent for two years where she acquired the rudiments of reading and writing, but spent most of her time embroidering. At the age of nine she returned home amid great rejoicing, and her education was henceforth directed by her father, Silvestro, a member of the Brescian aristocracy. About him we know nothing except that he was responsible for the fortifications of cities allied to Brescia. As a young girl, Laura accompanied her father on journeys to these cities supervising military construction. Her father's occupation presupposes a knowledge of mathematics. Laura herself was very early taken with this subject, which may have been due to his interest and knowledge. Her own interest was quickly translated also into a fascination with astrology, and her letters reveal a detailed knowledge of the zodiac and predictions to be derived therefrom. Her father taught her also Latin and Greek, and she concentrated especially on Latin eloquence. Very early Petrarch became her model, and she yearned to emulate him. Her interests turned from mathematics to moral philosophy, classical literature and sacred studies. These latter subjects became a consuming passion.

At the age of fifteen she was married to a Brescian businessman, Pietro Serina and, at the same time, began a literary correspondence in Latin with the learned of her city and, outside it, in the Veneto. She found time for her studies by writing after everyone else had gone to bed. Cereta is unique among the women we have discussed in this respect. Her studies did not cease but rather became more intense after she married. Whether the patterns of the lives of other learned women might have been repeated in her own life we cannot know, for her husband died of the plague after they had been married for only eighteen months, leaving her childless. After a period of intense grief during which she yearned for death, she recovered herself not, as she says, through weeping, but through the resumption of her literary labors. Even more zealously, she wrote letters to the learned and sought to enter into the world of humanism. Most of her correspondents were local Brescians, unknown to us except in her letters. But some were humanists who attained something of a reputation, for example, Bonifacio Bembo and Ludovico Cendrata. She also wrote to Cassandra Fedele. None of these better known correspondents replied to her, even though she asked explicitly that they do so. Perhaps they did not consider her significant enough.

Nonetheless, she became something of a phenomenon in Brescia itself, and her peers there certainly did not ignore her. They attacked her. Her male peers charged that her letters had been written for her by her father, because no woman could be learned enough to write such letters. To this she responded that she was pleased to have herself compared so favorably to her father, whom she admired, and then proceeded to demonstrate her erudition in response to one and all. She may also have been the only woman humanist of the century to use that genre of writing invented by Petrarch and his followers, the invective. Cereta penned one against two of her male peers that rivals in vitriol those of Filelfo, Poggio or Valla. Not only men but also women attacked her. To them she responded (selection 15) in a letter unique among learned women writers. She also wrote perhaps the best defense of the education of women to be found in humanist literature during the Quattrocento (selection 14).

Cereta was praised by other humanists as well as critized by her peers. She refers in many of her letters to the adulation others heaped upon her. But she saw through it in a way other learned women did not or, if they did, never publicly expressed. She recognized male flattery as condescension: to say that she was a learned woman and therefore unusual was to say something negative about women. Cereta was both perceptive and aggressive in her defense of women (selection 13).

In 1488 Cereta dedicated the first volume of her letters (the only one ever published) to Cardinal Maria Ascanio Sforza, hoping that his position would lend legitimacy to her work and that her work, in turn, would redound to his glory. Given the attitudes expressed in the letters of this volume, one might have expected much more from her pen. But she lived eleven more years without publishing anything further. Why such silence from a woman so determined, so perceptive, so positive about her self both as a woman and as a humanist?

The answer appears self-evident: she found no acceptance in the world of humanism, which remained a male preserve. Only one correspondent wrote letters to Cereta which are preserved, a Dominican Friar, Tommaso of Milan (selections 21 and 22). In them he upbraided her for taking her critics so seriously and, more especially, for responding to them in such strong language. In writing so, he believed, she reflected more a pagan than a Christian consciousness. He counseled her to turn away from her humanism to religion, not even to religious studies but to the religious life. Cereta had always found her strongest male supporter in her father. Six months after she published her first volume of letters he died. Bereft now of her strongest male affirmation, besieged all around by critics, male and female, rejecting her humanism, and counseled by her one male correspondent to give up her humanism, she succumbed. She never married again, and she did not enter the religious life. But she found a social role more acceptable to those about her than that of humanist intellectual, and her pen fell silent.

Alessandra Scala (1475–1506) was the daughter of Bartolommeo Scala (1428–97), a humanist in the circle that gathered around Lorenzo de' Medici in Florence during the 1470s and 1480s.[26] During his later years he served as chancellor of the city of Florence and, like his predecessors in that office, Leonardo Bruni and Poggio Bracciolini, wrote a history of the city. His daughter, Alessandra, thus had access to the highest literary circles of Florence. She was tutored in Greek by the Greeks Lascaris and Chalcondylas and in Latin literature by Angelo Poliziano. By all contemporary reports she was a very beautiful woman, and there have been speculations over whether epigrams written in her honor by her teachers, Lascaris and Poliziano, meant that they were in love with her. Be that as it may, Alessandra is unique among the women considered here by virtue of the fact that one of the two remaining products of her pen is a Greek epigram written in reply to one written for her by Poliziano. That she knew Greek very well is attested by Poliziano also, who says she recited perfectly in Greek Sophocles' play *Electra*. The only other writing of hers known to be extant is a letter to Cassandra Fedele (selection 16b).

In 1494 Alessandra married a Greek poet, Michele Marullo. We hear nothing of the continuation of her studies thereafter. He died tragically in 1500, and she retired to a convent where she died six years later.

## Patterns in the Lives of Women Humanists

A number of similarities in the lives of these women humanists emerge from the biographies just presented. All of them were from substantial, most from aristocratic, families in the urban centers of Northern Italy. All came from homes in which learning was valued; in many cases the tradition of learning in the family extended back several generations. In every case the learning of girls was strongly supported by their fathers. In at least two cases the fathers were the principal if not the only teachers; in other cases the fathers chose tutors who taught the young women, perhaps alongside their brothers.

In every case the women, as young girls, were encouraged and strongly supported in their studies. They were recognized by their families, by male humanists, and by their cities as prodigies. Those women, however, who aspired to continue a humanist career into their adult years were not greeted with the encouragement or praise they had received as prodigies, but icily and with hostility. There was simply no place for the learned woman in the social environment of Renaissance Italy. What was a young girl to do who had been encouraged, had excelled, and had grown to love studies enough to dream of a humanist vocation?

Two socially acceptable alternatives were open to women. One was marriage, the other religious vows. Many chose marriage, and of those who did, only one maintained her humanist studies intensely after marriage. Only one other (because of her long life) returned to her studies after the death of her husband. A number of others took religious vows, and some evidence suggests that they did so in order to be able to continue the pursuit of their studies, though we do not actually have anything from the pens of any of these women after they entered the convent. Only one woman neither took religious vows nor married, but attempted to hew out an independent position for herself, an attempt which can be judged only partially successful.

Many of the women considered died young. One died in childbirth. Several had illnesses which today would perhaps be diagnosed as psychosomatic, in some cases stemming from the conflict between personal desire and social necessity. In several cases, it is reasonable to regard the conflict generated by the desire to pursue a life of the mind and the obstacles in its way as a contributory cause of early death.

Most of the women considered were strongly interested in religion and religious studies. This emphasis, which we found in Bruni's letter to Battista Malatesta, pervades the century. The bond between religion and chastity, made evident in Antonio Loschi's encomium to Maddalena Scrovegni, was lived out in the lives of these learned women. Some entered a convent, perhaps, as we argue, to gain for themselves both physical and psychological liberty. Others undertook, in their own homes, lives of religious solitude. The religious life was a sphere in which women could pursue their studies without inviting criticism.[27]

## Assessment of the Work of the Women Humanists

Those relatively few women who had the opportunity to participate in humanist culture mastered its rudiments as well as did their male contemporaries. They became highly proficient Latin stylists, competent in Greek (some competent enough to write poetry in that language), knowledgeable enough in the literature of classical Greece, Rome, and Christianity to fill their works with quotations and allusions to major and minor writers in each of those traditions.

In all the works of the humanists of whatever genre there was much that was imitative, conventional, repetitive. There was much affectation in their language and in the way they addressed those of higher station than themselves. They also had an inflated sense of the importance of what they wrote, especially in their view that by virtue of writing or dedicating a translation to someone, they were conferring immortality both on the person addressed and on themselves. This sense of their own importance is reflected as well in the invectives they invented, for they believed that vilifying an enemy had as much effect in casting the person into oblivion as praise and deference in rendering her or him immortal. The women considered here did not escape these common vices of humanist writers. Indeed, it would be very surprising if they had.

But just as they did not escape the vices of humanist writing, they shared in its merits. They were effective public speakers, as Part I of this anthology testifies, using their learning in behalf of their cities or their families. They discussed with acumen and interest a number of issues that characterize humanist literature and one that is peculiar to themselves, on which Part II largely focuses. And they received the recognition of their male peers and teachers, as reflected in Part III, though with some peculiar implications already discussed.

Part II of this anthology shows that there was one important respect in which learned women differed from their male contemporaries: they had to spend much of their limited energy defending their role as women humanists. Isotta Nogarola defends Eve, Laura Cereta writes against women whose primary interest is ornamentation, defends the liberal instruction of women and chastises men whose praise of women is really disguised condescension. Cassandra Fedele addresses the question posed by Alessandra Scala whether she should pursue learning or get married. It is important to recognize that males did not have to face such issues. Men who spent time on other pursuits were not a threat to men of learning. The latter simply ignored them or, if they were wealthy, perhaps sought their patronage. Nor would it ever have occurred to a male to argue that boys should be instructed in the liberal arts. Men in this social class could assume this as a right or even a duty. Similarly, men did not pause to consider whether there was a conflict between the desire to be a humanist and marriage.[28] Male humanists married, some of them several times. Some also had illegitimate children. But such behavior presented no conflict in their lives as humanists. Their personal lives were unimportant. But for women there was no such separation between vocational intellectual roles and social roles. This problem is still with us: women still must often choose between vocation and family. Men are rarely confronted with the necessity of such a choice.

Most of the literature produced by women is secular, which is not at all to say that it is anti-religious or impious, but only that religion was not their primary concern as humanists. This is quite remarkable, for if one looks at what men wrote to learned women (Part III) one sees the strong emphasis placed on the virtues of pursuing the religious life. In contrast, men seldom wrote to other men about the virtues of pursuing the religious life. Indeed, male humanists sometimes wrote against the religious life or, at least, about its pitfalls and hypocrisy. Only with respect to women, and for reasons already discussed, was learning pushed in the direction of religion.

But though this stress on religion by men had little effect on what learned women wrote, it probably had a great deal on what they did not write. It may well have been the ultimate intention of men to *divert* learning *into* religion, but whether this intention can be imputed to men or not, the effect was the same, for women, once they became convinced that they should enter the religious life or preoccupy their lives with matters of religion, ceased to be productive writers. Their pens were as much silenced by religion as they were by marriage.

Judged by the productions of their male contemporaries, the works of the women considered in this anthology are fairly successful. The greatest male humanists wrote works surpassing these in quality. But most of the work of most humanists does not fall into the category of superior thought or originality. The women compare favorably with much that humanism produced, though not with the best that humanism produced.

This conclusion is only what one would expect given the lives of the women humanists recounted earlier. Regarded as prodigies when they were young, they were forced either into the convent or into marriage when they grew to adulthood, both of which had the effect of stifling their intellectual development. Many show a promising start and some real achievement, but none (with the partial exceptions of Isotta Nogarola and Cassandra Fedele) was able to mature. Most, in fact, died very young and, in any case, virtually all that we have from their pens was produced when they were very young.

One has to conclude that women both were oppressed and oppressed themselves. Denied participation in the world of the male intellectual, they came to accept the low self-image of their femininity provided them by males. This, together with the social pressures to conform to social roles acceptable for women, was too much to withstand. The learning which made many of these women so happy as young girls made them miserable as women.

## The Heritage of the Women Humanists of the Renaissance

Humanism in Italy was largely a movement of the fifteenth century. During the following century Italian intellectual life, as its political life, took other directions. But there is, even so, evidence that the woman humanist made an impact upon her culture. She did not achieve great status in the world of humanism or recognition of intellectual parity with men. Yet her accomplishment was significant. By engaging in the humanist movement, she surpassed her medieval forebears and most of her contemporaries in other parts of Europe.[29] Moreover, she transmitted to the next centuries an important heritage: the notion that women could participate creatively as intellectuals in the shaping of culture.

That notion was successfully conveyed to all of Europe in Castiglione's immensely popular *The Courtier*. Book III outlines a social role for women, apart from that of nun or wife, as vital participant in the life of the court.[30] To fulfill this role, while she is not encouraged to be a thinker herself, the court lady requires an intensive education. She is not a proud and independent figure—an Isotta Nogarola or Laura Cereta—but she is their successor.[31]

There is also, in Italy, evidence of new behavior patterns among learned women. This is noticeable in the cases of three well-known poets, Vittoria Colonna (1490–1547), Gaspara Stampa (1520/1525–1554) and Veronica Franco (1546–90). Colonna was married for a few years but separated from her husband even during most of her married years. She wrote poetry both during his life and after his death and became the center of a literary circle that included a number of the most learned men of her generation. She also became a close spiritual friend of Michelangelo's. Stampa fell in love with a man above her in social class, with whom she had an affair but by whom she was cast off after three years. She wrote about this event with passion in her poetry and even sought other experiences (and wrote other poetry) after this one had been concluded. Franco was a courtesan in Venice, much sought after by highborn men. Her portrait was painted by, among others, Tintoretto. Although converted from her life as courtesan, she composed a good deal of love poetry, frankly passionate and sensual. In all three women we see something new in relation to the fifteenth-century women humanists. They were not shackled by the bonds of matrimony, they did not accept the customary roles for women, and they continued to write throughout their lives. At the same time, what they wrote—largely love poetry—represented a significant narrowing of the field of women's expertise.

The learned humanist woman moved from Italy to Northern Europe with the movement of humanism itself and, in part also, with the Protestant Reformation.[32] In his colloquy "The Abbot and the Learned Lady," written for the March 1524 edition of his *Colloquies*, Erasmus contrasts the idea of the abbot that a woman should pay attention only to dinner parties, external honors, and French novels, with the wise and learned Magdalia. To the comment that the public knows it is rare for a woman to know Latin, she responds that the public is the worst authority on conduct, that the fruits of learning, unlike other things that human beings create, will accompany us to the next life, and that as priests become increasingly more stupid the women may one day assume the reins of responsibility. She cites the More girls in England (Magdalia is inspired by Margaret More Roper) and the Pirckheimer and Blauer girls in Germany as exceptionally learned, and points out that in Spain and Italy as well there are not a few women who can rival any man in learning.[33] Willibald Pirckheimer, imperial councilor, humanist and friend of Erasmus, had five learned daughters. Margaret Blauer of Constance was said to have been a good Latinist (her two brothers were known to Erasmus). And of course Erasmus knew the More girls—Margaret, Cicely, and Elizabeth. Margaret, Sir Thomas More's favorite, married William Roper, who admired her learning, and she translated Erasmus' exposition of the Lord's Prayer from Latin into English.

During the same year in which Erasmus wrote this colloquy, Vives published his work, *On the Education of the Christian Woman*, in which the notion of the equality of men and women in learning is accepted as a starting point.

There is one great difference between Castiglione on the one hand and Erasmus and Vives on the other in their affirmation of the capacity for learning in men and women and in their acceptance of a role for the learned woman: Castiglione was speaking of the court lady, Erasmus and Vives of the middle class woman. Antronius the monk says to Magdalia in Erasmus' colloquy that "it is fitting for court ladies to have something with which to beguile their leisure," to which Magdalia replies: "Are court ladies the only ones allowed to improve their minds and enjoy themselves?"[34] Not only was the capacity for learning in both sexes affirmed, but it was filtering down into the now prosperous middle classes. The woman humanist in fifteenth-century Italy thus came at a propitious moment in the history of Western culture. She is now everywhere among us, and we owe her presence in part to the discipline, struggle, and suffering of her fifteenth-century predecessors, a glimpse of whose immaculate hand is here offered for the first time in a modern language.

# Part I

# Women
# in the
# Public Arena

# I

## Letter of the Lady Maddalena,
### Daughter of the Lord Ugolino degli Scrovegni of Padua, to the lord Jacopo dal Verme, Rejoicing in the conquest of Padua by the Lord Count of Virtues, etc., which she wrote with her own hand

## Introduction

Maddalena Scrovegni (1356–1429) was the first of the well-known learned women of the Quattrocento. The letter translated here is important because it indicates that even in the earliest years of humanism, women were drawn into the movement.[1]

Maddalena was born and grew up in Padua. She married in 1376, but her husband died after a short time, and she returned to her native city (1381). Padua at this time was caught in the struggle for power between Venice and Milan. The Carrara family ruled Padua, but they were being challenged by the Scaligeri who ruled Verona and Vicenza. On October 18 and 21, 1387, these two cities ceded control to the Visconti of Milan. Ugolotto Biancardo, a cousin of Maddalena's, was the Visconti governor of Vicenza. The Scrovegni abandoned the Carrara whom they had supported and went over to the Visconti, who now set their sights for Padua. By November 24, 1388 a Visconti garrison under Biancardo held the citadel in Padua. By December 18, the city was taken by Jacopo dal Verme. At the suggestion of Biancardo, Maddalena wrote the letter here translated to dal Verme, congratulating him on the conquest of the city. The victory, it might be added, was short-lived. The Carrara soon resumed control of the city and the Scrovegni family was forced to flee. Maddalena spent the rest of her life in Venice, exiled from her native Padua.

The Latin of this letter is not as clear as that of later humanists. We have attempted to grasp its essential meaning rather than translate literally. One might note also the absence of classical citations or allusions. All quotations are from the Bible. Later women humanists will emphasize much more the classical literary traditions of Greece and Rome.

This translation is based on the Latin text edited by A. Medin, "Maddalena degli Scrovegni e le discordie tra i Carraresi e gli Scrovegni," in *Atti e Memorie della Regia Accademia di scienze, lettere ed arti in Padova*, 12 (1896): appendix, 260–62.

## Text

THOUGH TOO BOLD, YET MOVED by the plea of that brave man, the Lord Ugolotto, my [cousin], I, of inferior sex, have set out to write to you, most glorious hero, worthy of reverence for your multitudinous virtues, now that you have enjoyed success as usual. I recall these verses of David's: "Sing to the Lord a new song, because he has done wonderful things!"[2] "The Lord has made known his salvation, in the sight of the nations he has revealed his justice."[3] "He stooped down to me, and he heard my cry. He drew me out of the pit of destruction, from the mire of the swamp, and he set my feet upon a rock."[4] "And he put a new song in my mouth."[5] "Rejoice to God our helper,"[6] happy and truly blessed citizens, since the world's most brilliant light which you have longed for has just dawned on your wretched city, and calmed it. The cloud of calamity has been lifted under heaven's serene majesty. A glorious star has appeared to us, sent by God from heaven, delightful in brilliance, radiant in justice and piety, the notable ornament of a higher realm, which we, kneeling, should, in my opinion, venerate and revere. By this venerable sign, as though having a steady oarsman, we should direct our course of pleasant prosperity through the open sea of life. In this way we may at last, having been tossed about on the many vile waves of a hostile storm, select a safe port on shore and, anchoring our ship, escape shipwreck. Our rudder shall be guided by the clemency of our most serene and glorious Lord Prince, who will place a check on bold sinners and compel miscreants to seize their rewards and make their harsh sceptres give out mournful songs. For by his bright power, the shameless tyrants have already begun to stumble and perish, to suffer an evil fate by death. They have hastened across the fields in the depravity of their crimes, and run up against the sentence of divine judgment, unaware that evil men's evil deeds will meet with evil dues and be trampled underfoot with awful reproaches. They are sunk in the profound stupor of the eternal night of their crimes, thus calling upon themselves fitting punishment for their perfidy. Such perfidy, contrary to its desired end, often quickly brings itself to ruin so that the guilt one places upon another one suffers for oneself. Where iniquities arise, there indeed they find their end, and heinous sins return to their authors. Therefore I may "rejoice because of thy help," God, since "the nations have fallen into the pit which they dug,"[7] "for their works follow them."[8] "Salvation and glory and power belong to our God, for true and just are his judgments."[9] O true judgments of God, measured with just calculation and proper weight! For what more miserable, more calamitous, more unhappy thing could befall a cruel tyrant than that, with the approval of all, he should be thrown down from his lofty peak and proud throne to the depths of wretched desolation, so that he understand that "God will destroy thee, he will remove thee forever; he will draw thee out of thy tent and he will uproot thee from the land of the living. The just shall see and fear, and shall laugh at him: 'Behold the man who made not God his fortification, but trusted in the abundance of his riches and gathered strength by his crimes.' "[10] But, finally, while sceptres fall and, in a flash, fierce empires are shattered, themselves ruined along with those they had oppressed, in the frenzied rush of punishment, may God, "reward them according to their works and according to the malice of their crimes. Give to them according to the work of their hands, render to them their due."[11] You say: "I will set judgment in weight, and justice in measure,"[12] [and the multitude of all nations] "shall be as the dream of a vision by night."[13] Indeed, those wicked magnates vanish into nothingness, and finally their crimes are punished. Surely anyone who prepares a place of retribution is also preparing the place of his own downfall, because the evil, unaware, inflict evil on themselves in their thirst for evil. Nothing should be more greatly feared than the miserable infliction of terrible cruelties. Farewell. I, a woman of uncultivated mind, revere you without ceasing and recommend myself to your excellence.

Magdalena de Scrovegni,
written by her own hand,
as best she knows how, in Padua

2

### Oration of Battista da Montefeltro Malatesta to the Emperor Sigismund

### Introduction

Sigismund, to whom this oration was delivered, had been king of Hungary since 1387, a position he retained until his death in 1437. In 1411 he was elected Holy Roman Emperor and shortly thereafter played a leading role in the Council of Constance. He was instrumental in getting Pope John XXIII to attend the Council where, on Christmas Eve, 1414, the pope recognized Sigismund as Holy Protector. This came to nothing, however, since John himself was soon deposed (with the help of Sigismund who withdrew his support) and fled the Council. In 1431

Sigismund once again attempted to seek papal acknowledgement of his office and
went to Italy with the intention of having himself crowned by the pope as Holy
Roman Emperor. But after receiving some honors in Lombardy, he was not wel-
comed elsewhere—the Florentines refused him permission to pass through their
territory—and he remained secluded in Siena for six months before retreating back
across the Alps. Shortly afterwards, however, Sigismund returned to Italy again
and finally was crowned Holy Roman Emperor by Pope Eugenius IV on May
31, 1433. On his way to Rome he stopped in Urbino, where Battista delivered
this oration before him.

Battista was married in 1405 to Galeazzo Malatesta, heir to the lordship of Pesaro.
He assumed this position in 1429 but after two years of despotic rule was
assassinated. In her first petition, Battista refers to his deposition and asks the restora-
tion of Pesaro to her family.

The situation she describes in the remainder of the oration is intimately tied
to the history of the Varano family, to which Battista was related through the
marriage of her daughter. The Varano family were lords of Camerino. But shortly before this oration was delivered, the four Varano brothers who ruled
Camerino—Giovanni II, Gentile Pandolfo, Berardo, and Pier Gentile—began a
fratricidal war to gain exclusive control, each for himself. Pier Gentile, the husband of Battista's daughter, was imprisoned; at least one of his brothers was killed
during the time he was in prison (his death is referred to by Battista). The deaths
of the others were to follow shortly, but not before (and perhaps through their
intrigue) Pier Gentile was killed in prison (September 6, 1433) by the pope's general,
Giovanni Vitelleschi.[1] Battista's pleas, therefore, in retrospect, were to no avail.
Her son-in-law was not saved by Sigismund. Her daughter, as she says at the end
of her oration, was left with four small children. We shall meet them again in
the introduction to the next selection.

This translation is based on the Latin text published by G. B. Mittarelli, *Bibliotheca
codicum manuscriptorum Monasterii Sancti Michaelis Venetiarum prope Murianum*
(Venice, 1779), pp. 701–2.

## *Text*

H ERE IN THE VERY PRESENCE of your Serenity, most Christian Emper-
or, I would have long stood not only speechless at the beginning
of my crude oration, but nearly paralyzed, had I not, remembering
your generosity, recognized you as our lord, our leader, sent us from heaven.
But your kindness and the sincere devotion of our house to your sublimity
manages to vanquish the greatness of that awe. For since God has lent divinity to your countenance, I hope to find there divine aid and mercy, and in
you a willing listener. While I have no power of speech, no means of persuasion, yet by the grace of your ancestors and of your present greatness, our
whole family is utterly devoted to your majesty. Relying on this occasion,

therefore, both on your imperial benignity and the privilege [accorded me by] my devotion, and strengthened by your sacred Majesty's permission, I shall proceed, even if inelegantly, to what I wish to say. But first, I—among the least of your handmaidens—commend your surely unprecedented piety in accepting your crown from the true and holy Pope, for whose sake you as emperor will heal and reform an Italy ripped to shreds, as unwavering justice shines forth from your throne. You will restore to their position those unjustly ruined. Among their number is my magnificent lord Galeazzo, and his magnificent brothers, who should not be dismissed as less than wholly faithful to you, who, having been expelled from their own homes and despoiled of the dominion which they had justly ruled and mercifully governed, are now afflicted with trouble and calamity. Do not suppose, triumphant prince, that this happened to them because of any cruelty toward their subjects or any oppression of them or any kind of cause; rather, it happened because of the prideful violence of a few arrogant citizens who would not condescend even a little to bend their necks to a sweet-tempered lord, to the yoke of merciful rule, and treacherously turned the city of Pesaro to rebellion. On this account an unhappy populace, lacerated by intestine war and domestic strife, has been lured into great chaos. For many were sentenced to exile, others were despoiled of all their goods, other tortured in prisons, others were hanged, suffering death's sting.[2] Thus depopulated, the city suffered in the end such damage that the elegant tongue of Demosthenes would falter in describing it.[3] But since these disastrous events were reported to you by your magnificent sister, the lady Victoria, and by others loyal to you, I shall not dare to smite your kind ears further in their narration. I could briefly mention the violated tomb of my lord and father, and the remains of orthodox princes savagely mutilated. But yet I cannot go further; for tears would erupt ahead of my words; my throat is choked by indignation and pain alike.

By your innate clemency, therefore, pious Augustus, open the bosom of your ample love to these devoted children, born of the famous Malatesta lineage, longing for your protection; and before you leave Italy, put an end to so much anguish and violence. This is my first petition to your unvanquished Majesty; I have asked it incited by the unshaken hope that my devotion will not go unrewarded by your Majesty.

Finally, something exceedingly, overwhelmingly bitter (which, when I reflect upon it, causes enormous disturbance of mind) recently happened, Serene Prince, to your devoted son and dedicated servant Pier Gentile da Camerino, the husband of my only daughter, whom Count Richard humbly entrusted to you on my behalf. It would befit your imperial soul both to protect him and, among other things, to care and provide for him as much as possible. For you are aware of the horrible crime, the violent and tragic murder of his brother. I add the unexpected capture of my son. For you know, most clement of princes, he is held in prison, bound in fetters, by the governor of the Marches. I shall not comment on the manner of his capture, I shall remain silent about the ransom for his well-being; only I beg your Majesty that you extend to this wretched calamity your pious hands, and strive to release from the dark servitude of prison my innocent son, most loyal to your command, so that, restored to his original liberty, he may know that in harsh misfortunes Caesar's clemency, in which, after God, is his greatest hope, has never failed.

Among the nearly innumerable blows which afflict my unhappy lord is the thought of his wife, left alone, an unfortunate girl with four small children, despoiled of all her fortune and wealth, with not even a robe left her, except that one alone which she was wearing when captured. And at present the castle in which she is confined is guarded by mercenaries who favor her brother and persecute her innocent child. Therefore, I pray you, most excellent of princes, that you ask from the Pope this favor: that my son-in-law, rather son, may be returned to me by your help and assistance, and an end made to so horrible a war; that his wife with her children may lead their lives at least in peace, though in poverty, and you will have innumerable people who will praise your fame forever. Your generosity, most pious Emperor, has tolerated my inept speech, not disdaining my words which lack both elegance and grace. I pray and entreat the Lord Jesus Christ that he who gave you to us as our monarch on earth, a monarch decorated with a wondrous radiance of virtues, continue to grant you good health in accordance with our prayer.

## 3

### Oration of Costanza Varano
### to Bianca Maria Visconti,
### most illustrious and excellent of ladies

## Introduction

When the fratricidal strife of Camerino led to the murder of Pier Gentile, the father of Costanza Varano, Costanza's mother, the daughter of Battista da Montefeltro Malatesta, escaped the city with four young children, among whom were her own son Rodolfo, her daughter Costanza, and Giulio Cesare, the son of another of the murdered brothers, Giovanni II. She went to Pesaro, the home of Pier Gentile, and there raised the children. It was in Pesaro that Costanza received her education, following in the tradition of her grandmother, Battista Malatesta. In 1444 Alessandro Sforza married Costanza. Alessandro was the brother of Francesco Sforza, destined to become the Duke of Milan in 1450. For in 1441 Francesco had married Bianca Maria Visconti, the heir to her father, Filippo Maria Visconti, ruler of Milan until his death in 1447. Francesco at this time (1444) controlled the city of Camerino, and when his brother married Costanza, he returned the city to Varano control, reinstating Rodolfo, Costanza'a brother, and Giulio Cesare (then only twelve years old). The family maintained peace in Camerino until Cesare Borgia took it in 1502.

The occasion for this speech, then, is the return of the city of Camerino to the Varano family. Costanza, apparently prior to her marriage but in the same year, 1444, delivered this oration before Bianca Maria, requesting the cession of Camerino. The oration attests not only her learning but that of Bianca Maria as well. The marriage doubtless had more to do with the return of the city to Varano rule, however, than did Costanza's oration.

This translation is based on the Latin text edited by J. Lamius, *Catalogus codicum manuscriptorum qui in Bibliotheca Riccardiana Florentiae adservantur. . . .* (Livorno, 1756), pp. 146–47.[1]

## Text

WITHOUT A DOUBT, THE HEAVIEST BURDEN I could imagine – disproportionate to my strength – has been laid on my slim shoulders, most illustrious and excellent of ladies. For what oratorical flair, what richness of speech can I muster from my jumbled store of words so little suited to the task, [to praise] your nobility, wisdom, dignity, piety, most kind generosity, and other virtues? In such a matter, not only would a plain, uncultivated and girlish speech be insufficient, but even the spirits of the wisest men and most brilliant orators would flag; and, what is more, even the unvanquished and lush oratory of the most eloquent Cicero would collapse and fail.[2] What, therefore, can I do, an ignorant, rough, and inexperienced girl? Even though I tremble both in mind and body, and a blush stops my mouth from speaking freely, [still], may I say, the stones of this palace will proclaim your praise. But enough! I shall be steadfast and describe to the limit of my strength your very bright, lofty, and nearly divine virtues, though they have no need of such a humble celebration. But I must confess my inadequacy and slight skill in speaking; and if your great generosity, clemency and courtesy had not conferred hope and faith on me [isolated here], my soul would draw back, my lips would hesitate, my tongue, limp and stammering, would fall silent.

I am well aware of the widespread renown of your name, which has with such virtues adorned this most noble Italy of ours—and not only Italy but the circumference of the whole earth. You are famed, indeed, for having surpassed all excellent ladies of Latium[3] in birth, nobility, and fineness of character. For there is no one, no matter how wild, how barbarous his character, how alien and remote the country of his birth, who would not flame with the fire of the love of your many virtues. Oh happy Italy, who from her womb has given birth to such a radiant light! Oh how fortunate is your glorious and excellent spouse! Oh how blessed also are all those who are privileged to be among your company! Trusting your kindness, therefore, by which I shall be forgiven if anything I utter be flawed, incomplete or inelegant, with all my timidity set aside, I shall undertake to set forth briefly that [favor] I wish [from you].

So worthy, so excellent and noble is the deed [I wish you to perform], demonstrating such piety and winning such glory through virtue that the corrosion of countless centuries could not destroy it; nothing greater, nothing more useful, nothing more excellent can be conceived. For what could be a more excellent kind of piety than to restore to his proper princedom one who, because of his love for that just and glorious prince, your father, lost his ancient and rightful throne? You indeed, I know, are aware that the magnificent and honorable father of my only brother Rodolfo, your servant, came from the Varano family. He ruled so virtuously and earnestly and was joined by such love and by the bond of charity to your illustrious and most powerful father that [the latter's] praises always flowed from the [former's] sweet speech. For that reason he, though innocent, suffered the torment of an undeserved and atrocious death. Whence it happened that we were at once orphaned of our noble father and expelled from our kingdom; and shortly before he fell asleep in the Lord, [our father] bequeathed to that same most excellent prince, your father, the Duke of Milan, his aforenamed son, so that he might bestow upon one whom he loved in life a precious treasure in death. For this reason, I, a suppliant, plead for your clemency and ask you to favor—which is the most easy for your Excellence to do—your servant Rodolfo Varano, who suffers the burdens of exile as a result of dutiful devotion and, moreover, has lost an honorable parent. I have not meant to suggest that you would stain your [record of] rare and unique benevolence with the charge of impiety; may it be far from you that anyone should suspect this. For you have that glorious and most excellent husband Francesco Sforza, who shines with such prudence and wisdom and with such arts of war and peace that he surpasses not only all the kings of his age but the reputation of those in the past [as well]. And I am accustomed often, as the Orator says, to place before my eyes, and with frequent speeches to observe, all the great deeds of our emperors, of foreign nations and most powerful peoples, and of famous kings.[4] These could not be compared to his in the magnitude of contests [entered upon] nor in the number of battles [fought], nor in the [number] of regions [traversed], nor in the willingness to face the enemy, nor in the [variety] of wars. Nor has anyone crossed remote lands more quickly than he, his march, I say, [unmarred] by defeat, but adorned with victories. He possesses, however, something [still] more excellent, that is, qualities of soul which neither the mutability of fortune nor human strength has the power to weaken: humanity and matchless clemency.

Now, therefore, I beg and pray, with the most earnest prayers I can, that you will not disdain to intercede on behalf of wretches [with him] who by a simple affirmative word can with his magnamity restore the throne of Camerino to his servant, my aforementioned beloved brother. I hope and trust that what you wish to do you will easily accomplish. On both of you we have now laid all the foundations of our hope. If you do this, you will deservedly win perpetual and immortal glory with men and God.

4

*Oration to the people of Camerino,*
*delivered to them by Costanza Varano*

## Introduction

This oration was delivered a short time after the preceding selection. The circumstances will be familiar from the introduction to that oration.

This translation is based on the Latin text edited by Lamius, *Catalogus*, pp.
145–46.[1]

## Text

I HAVE NEVER YEARNED SO MUCH with all my soul and strength for knowledge of letters and a refined eloquence in speech as I do at this moment,
illustrious citizens and excellent fathers. For now we see that day made
so glorious by your magnanimity, wisdom and humanity, that day so
unimaginable, so long-awaited, on which I would like to have not my slight
speaking skill, but that superlative and almost divine eloquence of Demosthenes,[2]
so that I could convey to all posterity with worthy praise and elegant words
your abundant merits, and the dignity, glory and triumph of this famed city,
which has surpassed all the cities of Italy in mercy, kindness and clemency.
Yet I quake and tremble not a little, and grow irritated at myself, for I realize
that I, ignorant and inexperienced, am in no way adequate for so serious and
important a task: for my meagre intellect is weak, and I have scarcely begun
my studies of letters and eloquence. But why do I say "begun"? I have not
even deserved to approach the first gateway to erudition. Yet, dear fathers,
the sight of you here restores and renews me, [bespeaking] your prudence,
charity, inexhaustible good will, and undaunted faith, which were evidenced
today to all of Italy, to the glory of your name, when you with one voice
recalled the magnificent lords, my loving brothers Rodolfo and Giulio Varano,
and [our whole family], to the rightful, proper, and ancient [throne] of our
ancestors. Therefore, with strengthened spirit I presume on your prudent and
humane natures, put aside the timidity of my girlish age, and attempt as vigorous-
ly as I can to extol and celebrate your unmatchable virtue—which should be
consecrated to eternal memory—with my pale words, quivering tongue, and
confused speech. For I judge that it is better [to bear accusations] of ignorance
and awkwardness than to be darkened with the black charges of detestable
ingratitude and churlishness.

Through many long years this glorious city of ours was considered outstanding among the others of the Picene plain: abundant in wealth, illustrious for
knowledge, powerful in arms, and imbued with civic virtue. But as of today,
she can rightly be compared not only to those other excellent cities of the
Marches and of Italy which respect the divine rule of princes (though for the
sake of brevity it is necessary to pass them by in silence), but even to that
most famous city of all Greece, Constantinople, which always chose to venerate
the sceptres of its emperors—even when the imperial rule was for a brief time
interrupted and then restored.[3] Now, Aristotle, the prince of philosophers,
records in his book of *Ethics* (which you even when asleep know better than
I when awake) that there are three forms of rule [found] in the world.[4] [Of
these] surely the least satisfactory is rule by the people; the second is rule by
many citizens outstanding in virtue; the best, however, and far more worthy
than all others, as Aristotle justly shows, is rule of kings and princes—that form
of rule which, when it had been lost through adverse fortune, you, with one
will and heart, by your skill and wisdom, reestablished. No one would be able
to obtain greater praise by any human skill than that praise which you have
obtained in recent days for the goodness of your hearts. As the Orator says
in the *Marcellus*, there is nothing made by hand and labor which age does
not eventually diminish or consume.[5] Yet your justice and fineness of soul
flowers more each day, so that whatever the passing of time takes from your
works, that much will it add to your praise.

The fruitful and flourishing field of your virtues unfolds, making it nearly
impossible not only to comprehend so much greatness in so few words, but
even to decide where to begin extolling your virtues. To do these things would
require not the brief space of this naïve oration, but the massive volumes of
the learned ancients. But compelled by the limitations of time, I intend to bring
my oration to a close, lest I appear to batter your gentle ears with my homely
words—full, nonetheless, with love and kindness. To you, loving citizens, the
illustrious and powerful prince, our lord and father the noble Galeazzo de'
Malatesta, and his magnificent consort, the ornament of all ladies, and our
sweet [grandmother], Lady Battista, together with our magnificent and noble
[mother] Lady Elizabeth, and the magnificent lords my brothers Rodolfo and
Giulio, and all of us of the Varano family, for your so great and unmatched
act of faith, offer eternal and ineffable thanks, and know that we owe you
even greater thanks than this. Nor do we alone thank you, but all the princes
and lords of Italy who are joined to us through either blood or good will.
Human capacity is not great enough to pay you sufficient rewards appropriate
to your merits. Wherefore may God remedy the defect of my inadequacy
and give to your reverences what your good deeds merit, and establish this
good people, free from all adversities, in a placid and tranquil peace. Finally,

we who have been given by you so clear a title of sovereignty, firmly promise, and with intact faith assure, that we shall be prompt to fulfill your just wishes and shall always venerate you not as citizens but as fathers. Farewell.

## 5

### Ippolita Sforza in honor of her mother, Bianca Maria, The Duchess of Milan

## Introduction

One year after Costanza Varano delivered her oration in honor of Bianca Maria Sforza, Ippolita was born to that princess. When Ippolita's father, Francesco, became Duke of Milan in 1450, he established a school for the education of his children, so that Ippolita, like Cecilia Gonzaga, may have received her humanist education in a school with her brothers and sisters, not at the hands of one or more private tutors. This address in honor of her mother was delivered prior to her marriage to Alfonso, Duke of Calabria, in 1465. She was at the time about twenty years of age.

Bianca Maria, as already recounted, was the daughter of Filippo Maria Visconti and was married to Francesco Sforza in 1441. Francesco was Filippo's general, but Filippo distrusted him and even besieged cities under his control. Bianca Maria remained loyal to her husband, defending his possessions against her father and supporting him even when he went over to the side of her father's enemies. Once established in Milan, she became a patron of the arts and supported the work of a number of humanists. Many of those she had encouraged took part in her funeral ceremonies, Francesco Filelfo pronouncing the funeral oration. She was also noted for many public works of charity, for which she was applauded by the people of Milan. An extremely competent woman, she assumed the reins of government in 1466 when her husband died, and she maintained control until her son, Galeazzo Maria, the heir, returned from France in 1468. He soon quarreled with her and she fled to Cremona, dying—rather suddenly—on the way. She certainly set a handsome example for Ippolita, who emulated her mother as Duchess of Calabria, patronizing men of letters and displaying great competence in her role.

This translation is based on the Latin text published by G. G. Meersseman, "La raccolta dell'umanista fiammingo Giovanni de Veris 'De arte epistolandi,' " *Italia medioevale e umanistica* 15 (1972): 250–51.

## *Text*

WHEN, MOST MAGNIFICENT PRINCESS, a great desire came over me to address something to you, I had to consider what would be worthy of your matchless love and pleasing charity toward me, and also befitting my affection and respect for you. Yet I have decided that there is no need for me to begin with a long introduction in order to arouse your good will. For nature brings it about [that mothers] not only see and hear their children gladly, but also nourish and educate them with every care and diligence and with great labor, so that posterity might remember and honor them; and nothing in life is dearer or more pleasant to them than the good health, virtue, and happiness of their children. I will speak plainly, then, most glorious princess, and my noble and honorable mother, and confess what I feel.

Now that I have finally arrived at that age at which I can have an understanding of moral principles, the more aware I am of your incredible and nearly divine virtue, and the more I feel that I bear upon my shoulders a weight heavier than Aetna[1] if, as befits a good daughter, I try to imitate and celebrate your most excellent virtues. Let me begin with those pertaining to religion. What pious princess ever in any age was more venerable or more saintly than you? Who more loving of Christ's poor or of holy men, who more dutiful in praying, fasting, and almsgiving, from which it appears more clear than the light of the sun that your immortal soul and beautiful heart are adorned to the full with theological virtues? For your intelligence shines resplendent with faith in the divine, your memory flowers with hopes of heaven, your will is inflamed and aglow with charity and the zeal of doing good for all humankind; for all these reasons your beautiful soul, created in the likeness of her creator, will attain eternal praise and glory. That is why there is in your prayers [rapt] contemplation of the eternal God and future beatitude. That is why there is in your fasts such [firm] abstinence from food and drink. That is why there is, finally, your great liberality and munificence towards all humankind, by which you build temples and chapels for the immortal gods. You enrich neighbors and relatives, you favor friends and well-wishers, you mercifully assist the poor with your wealth, so that you seem to have been born not for yourself alone but for the whole world.[2] For it appears to me, most magnificent mother, that none among your merits is more glorious or more excellent than this, that you willingly do good to many, and you confer your benefits most liberally upon every kind of person. For in liberality alone do princes seem to approx-

imate the power of God—when they, powerful and wealthy, lift up the pros-
trate, make erect the fallen, enrich the poor, make the rich even richer by
their liberality and munificence. Such are those whom we regard as kings and
whom we revere above men as gods.

But what may I say concerning your human character, your strength of soul,
your devotion to your mother, your goodness to your family, your justice
to all? For just as you were born to guide the king with your counsel, so by
cultivating those virtues you have learned how to bestow laws upon cities,
correct injustices, and by your prudence increase and glorify empire. For these
reasons, most excellent mother, I admire these virtues of yours, which I deem
should be praised and proclaimed, which I desire to pursue and imitate with
diligence and toil, by which I might also lift myself up from the earth and,
victorious, "fly through the mouths of men."[3]

# 6

## Oration of the illustrious Duchess of Calabria, daughter of the glorious Francesco, Duke of Milan, delivered to the Highest Lord Pope Pius in the Consistory of Cardinals, Mantua, 1459, in the month of July

## Introduction

Enea Silvio Piccolomini (1405–64), one of the leading humanists of his generation, was elected Pope Pius II in 1458. In 1453 the Christian Byzantine Empire
had come to an end with the capture by the Turks of Constantinople. The fall
of that city shocked the West. It was one of Pius II's dreams to restore Christendom in the East, and to this end he called a Congress at Mantua in 1459. In
terms of generating enthusiasm for a war against the Turks, the Congress was
a failure. Very few political leaders attended.

Among those who did, however, was Francesco Sforza, now Duke of Milan,
and his family. Pius II, who wrote a commentary on his times while pope, has
this to say about Francesco's family:

Pius entered Mantua on May 27, five days before the appointed date. The
city was full of guests and thronged with the people of the neighboring towns.

Among them was Bianca, Duchess of Milan, daughter of the late Duke Filippo Maria and wife of Francesco Sforza, a woman of high spirit and extraordinary wisdom. She had with her a most noble brood of children of both sexes, four boys beautiful as angels from heaven and a girl named Ippolita, lovely in face and character, who was betrothed to the son of the King of Sicily.[1]

Pius also comments that the next day "Bianca's daughter Ippolita delivered a speech before the Pope in such elegant Latin that all present were lost in wonder and admiration."[2] That would make the date of this oration May 28, although the heading says it was delivered in July. Since the heading was added later (Ippolita was not Duchess of Calabria when she delivered the oration), Pius' recollection is more probably correct.

The oration speaks of a petition, but this turns out to be nothing more than the commendation of her family to the Pope. What better way to commend a cultured and pious family than to have a fourteen-year-old girl represent the family with a Latin oration? For girls, if not for women, humanist learning had its utility.

This translation is based on the Latin text edited by C. Corvisieri, *Notabilia temporum di Angelo de Tummulillis da Sant'Elia*, Fonti per la storia d'Italia, vol. 7 (Livorno, 1890), pp. 231–33.[3]

## *Text*

SO GREAT, I HAVE OFTEN HEARD, is the authority and majesty of this holiest See, blessed [father], that no one, however intelligent, eloquent [or] worthy, has ever petitioned it who did not perform his task with trepidation. Certainly, then, I, who suffer shyness and timidity because of my age, sex and frailty of mind, am struck with fear, especially in the presence of such a judge as you, who are, by the consensus of all the worthiest men, most learned and wise. [Thus], blushing, I am silent not merely because of that blush, but because, indeed, I have not the courage to look upon your Holiness with unwavering eyes. But since I am also aware that you are good-natured, extraordinarily humane, benevolent, and merciful, and because I know it is holy to obey one's parents' commands, I shall undertake, bashfully and fearfully, the duty of speaking imposed on me. In a brief oration, I shall first explain the cause for our presence here, and then our petition.

When we learned that your Holiness had been exalted to this splendid throne, my illustrious parents and our whole family were suddenly overcome by such deep pleasure that nothing, I thought, could ever occur more contributory to our happiness, partly because of our family's great hopes, and partly, or rather particularly, for the sake of the general well-being of the Christian religion. For, indeed, we believe you are a star sent down from heaven to govern the bark of St. Peter [which is today] imperilled and nearly submerged. It augurs well, they feel, that [in these times when] Christendom is so endangered, you were chosen as the supreme pastor of the Lord's flock, not because of favor or privilege, but because of your lofty virtue and saintliness. But to what end do I dare to praise you? Is it in order to use my crude and childish words to make filthy your golden and nearly divine virtues? When we heard, then, that your Holiness had decided to set out for this city, my parents decided likewise to come too, to revere, worship [and] adore you; and since, consequently, I, too, am able to kiss your blessed feet, I feel I have experienced not a small, but a tremendous happiness. For since you are on earth the vicar of our Savior, we earthly mortals owe you much reverence and show you much obedience. I pray that you believe this: no one more zealously obeys or more ardently desires your prosperity and welfare, or the prosperity and welfare of the holy Roman Church, than my parents. And I, indeed, though I have no fortune of my own, both devote and dedicate my will, which is free, to your sanctity. It remains to be said only that my illustrious parents, my brothers, myself, our whole condition, I commend to your Holiness.

7

*Oration of Cassandra Fedele*
*to the Ruler of Venice, Francesco Venier,*
*on the arrival of the most serene Queen of Poland*

## Introduction

The most extraordinary thing about the oration translated below is that it was written and delivered by a woman ninety-one years of age. There is not a little irony involved here. For after her husband's death in 1521 Cassandra was reduced to poverty – his patrimony had been lost through an accident at sea. She suffered without assistance until, at the age of eighty-two, through the intercession of Pope Paul III, to whom she had appealed, the Venetian Senate appointed her prioress of the orphanage attached to the Church of San Domenico di Castello. She retained this positon until her death at the age of ninety-three. The Senate, which called her out of "retirement" to deliver this public oration, had not come to her assistance in her need, indeed, had forgotten the young woman who was such an ornament to the city that she had been refused permission to emigrate to Aragon in 1488.

This is therefore the latest work (1556) contained in this anthology, the only one that does not fall in the fifteenth century. Yet Cassandra really belongs to the fifteenth century. She was formed by the humanist program which developed then. The letter shows very well that she had not lost her Latin learning or eloquence in all the years when she (presumably) neglected her studies. It is interesting that she expresses the characteristic hope of humanism that writing about so distinguished a person will confer immortality on her.

This translation is based on the Latin text in *Cassandrae Fidelis Venetae, epistolae et orationes*, ed. J. F. Tomasini (Padua, 1636), pp. 207–10.

## Text

I F I WERE ABLE TO EXPRESS the great delight of the Venetian Senate in your longed-for arrival, serene and blessed Queen, I would say that the arrival of no other king or emperor has been more pleasing or agreeable, since no more pleasant or happier day has ever dawned upon this city than this one spent in greeting you joyfully.

Therefore, since I have been assigned by the Senate to describe to you not only its joy but also its benevolence toward you, and the pleasure and good will of the whole populace, I am grieved that I am unable to put in words or describe in my oration the great fullness of joy which dwells in my mind and heart. But these happy faces, these cheerful hearts, may amply convey to your majesty [what we feel]. For what lurks in our hearts you perceive clearly in our faces, as though shining through glass, and what you cannot hear because of the crudeness of this tongue you may hear in the cries of the people and see in the eyes of all, dancing, it seems, with joy. Thus all feel that the city should not only mark with a white pebble, as they say, this special day on which all have rejoiced, which you have brightened and indeed blessed with your benevolent glance, but celebrate it every year with highest honors.[1] Is there anyone so witless that he does not remember the most serene Queen of Poland? Who does not admire the greatness of her most holy and august presence? Who does not respect and venerate her as a divinity? This much I am able to say on behalf of all excellent [and] outstanding women: "Graceful deer will graze in heaven [before we forget this glorious day]."[2]

Certainly [the image of] the divine beauty of your mind and body will never escape from our heart, but the memory of your name will be so fixed in the minds of all that it will never be destroyed by the passage of time. I for my part, if I may speak personally, would so gladly spend all the days of my life celebrating the glory of your name—which, even if I were silent, spreads far and wide—that nothing more agreeable or desirable could befall me, not because

I think that you would receive any distinction from my writing and industry, but because I would hope that merely by honoring you, I also might be made immortal. But weighty age enfeebles my mind and prevents me from praising you [adequately] even though I want to, as I have long since been in retirement. But, insofar as it is possible at my age — and I think this will be no less dear and pleasing to you — I promise that I will always beseech the highest and greatest God for the greatness of your most fortunate kingdom, for long good fortune of body and mind. For the rest, this benevolent republic, having admired your distinguished gifts, the dowries as it were of your mind, kindly extends to you the highest honors, and celebrates you, a most holy queen, with a well-earned triumphal procession. For both your singular prudence in governing your peoples in the tranquillity of peace, and your wonderful fortitude of mind in the disturbances of wars (in which virtues you easily outstrip Thamyris, Queen of the Scythians, or Hypsicratea of Pontus), deserve this and much greater rewards.[3] But why does the dullness of this tongue, which daunts the highest will of mind and genius, not capture [in words] this quiet sea, this serenity of the air, this sweet and lightly blowing breeze, in obedience to our most worthy Senate? Who does not plainly see that your entrance into the bosom of this commonwealth will be so glorious that the heavens themselves, earth and sea, joyfully receive and celebrate [you] as Queen, and that not only the Senate and the Venetian people, but foreign peoples [as well] — all peoples of the earth — attend [you] with all honor.

# Part II

# Women on Women and Learning

# 8

*To the magnificent and glorious Lady Cecilia Gonzaga,*
*Costanza Varano sends greetings and salutes you*

## Introduction

This letter is something of a *tour de force*. The writer focuses her entire attention on her dilatoriness in writing, providing a variety of excuses: her rusticity, the sickness of her mother for whom she has to care, the death of the Archbishop of Patras which has caused her great sorrow. All of these excuses are meant at the same time to explain the poverty of her Latin style. Nonetheless, the excuses themselves are offered in the most florid Latin, certainly intended to demonstrate the opposite of what the letter actually asserts — a striking example of the triumph of form over content, characteristic of much writing by Renaissance humanists, both male and female.

The letter was probably written in 1444 prior to Costanza's marriage (December 8) and prior also to Cecilia's entry into a convent, of which no mention is made.

This translation is based on the Latin text edited by Lamius, *Catalogus*, p. 147. For another version, see the Bettinelli edition cited in "Book-Lined Cells," p. 83.

## Text

LTHOUGH I DISREGARDED MY GREAT ADMIRATION for your countless virtues, noble erudition, and unique eloquence, and instead preferred to pursue the great error of ambiguous silence or talkativeness, yet now, trusting in your prudence and in our mutual tie of consanguinity,[1] I finally have decided to put an end to my long silence. I realize that I have made a major mistake, and I admittedly deserve stinging reproof rather than kindly forgiveness. For I have [neglected to] nourish with frequent letters your benevolence, hope, and charity, which I have enjoyed from the cradle on, not because I have deserved them, but because you are kind. Yet it is necessary [to insure] that these charming virtues of yours not vanish from the recesses of your heart, but that they always firmly endure. Nor will the vast expanse of time ever cause me to lose the affection I feel toward you. But embarrassed by my own ignorance and clumsiness, and [aware] of your indescribable virtue and great knowledge of rhetoric, I did not write more quickly, and a considerable delay was occasioned. I hoped my work would become capable of a more ornate style; it was not so much that I wanted to conceal my rustic speech by speaking little, but that I wanted your gentle ears to hear letters written with a most lucid and clear eloquence. Certainly I feared to deafen them with my usual trivialities. But realizing that I am unable to write with enough art, I have thrown myself entirely into the arms of your humanity and have decided to write to your Highness this inelegant letter, full of spiritless words and disordered thoughts, lest you label me with all the titles of ingratitude regardless of how often in times past I had determined to discharge my epistolary duty. But the consuming weakness and poor health of my magnificent mother took my mind from those tasks [to the point where] my soul, tied up with cares and diverse anxieties, drew back from literary studies. Then on April 21, an unexpected, unintelligible, and tragic calamity occurred, the death, that is, of the dearest Father in Christ, D. D. Pandolfo, the Archbishop of Patras, by whose providence this very city was justly governed.[2] Whence it happened that, overcome by tears and inconsolable sorrow, I put letters behind me. My pen fell from my hand, and every thought was so barred from my mind that it became quite stripped of invention. Now, however, with newly resumed strength, I have been better able, I believe, to send you this letter composed utterly without beauty. I pass by in silence, then, your virtues so rare, so glorious, finally, so nearly divine. For they would demand not the brevity of a letter but the length of a book, as is expressed in this line of Virgil's: "Day would lie locked in heaven before the end!"[3] I see that I have wandered further than I first thought I would. For this reason, I have decided to put an end to my words, humbly praying and imploring you that if you find anything [in this letter] rough, unpolished, and unadorned, you will not disdain to render it improved and refined. If you will do this, I will be most pleased. Farewell.

# 9

*Costanza Varano sends greetings to Isotta Nogarola*

## Introduction

Costanza Varano is the only female admirer of Isotta Nogarola from whom a letter survives. The letter is notable in its praise both of Isotta's asceticism and of her learning.

Costanza makes reference to Isotta's self-imposed religious retreat (1441) when she says that Isotta has forsaken the needs of the body in reaching out for the immortal fame of the writer and scholar. She uses interesting language in making this point, asserting that it is more "fruitful" for women to forsake the needs of the body in seeking goods that fortune cannot destroy. Is she using the word ironically here? In any case, we must believe she was aware of the conflict between intellectual activity and the generativity usually associated with women. She cites Lactantius, Cicero, and Quintilian, who had praised those who rejected physical goods to live the life of the mind. Costanza understood that only through denial of the body could a woman achieve the intellectual goals Isotta sought.

Costanza's praise of Isotta is extravagant. Isotta is related to an historical chain of learned women through the ages, some of whom are named. Even more strikingly, in a poem accompanying this letter (not translated), she is said to surpass even the most learned men of her age.[1] No man ever honored Isotta for this (though Angelo Poliziano later praises Cassandra Fedele in such terms: selection 23). Isotta is clearly perceived as a model for those women who aspire to intellectual achievement. But her life is also a testimony to the price exacted for it: self-imposed isolation and denial of sexuality. It was not a path designed to draw very many into its orbit!

The probable date of the letter is 1443 or 1444.

This translation is based on the Latin text in *Isotae Nogarolae Veronensis opera quae supersunt omnia . . .*, ed. E. Abel, 2 vols. (Vienna and Budapest, 1886), 2:3–6. Other versions of the text may be found in the editions of Varano's works by Lamius and in Bettinelli, cited in "Book-Lined Cells," p. 83.

## Text

AFTER I HAD READ REPEATEDLY YOUR ELEGANT LETTERS, most learned Isotta, letters redolent of that ancient dignity of the Romans, letters in which the embellishments are as suited to the thoughts as to the words, I became aware of how much I am affected with love for you, [and I was] moved by your eloquence to tell you so in my letter, although my words are unpolished, partly because of the poverty of my mind and partly because of the inadequacy of my training in eloquence. But why do I speak of training when I have scarcely begun the first lesson? Hence I congratulate you, for you have advanced to the highest peaks, to the great splendor and glory of your name. For nothing could be more expedient and fruitful for women than to forget the needs of the body and to reach out strenuously for those goods which fortune cannot destroy. You have obeyed from earliest infancy that injunction of Lactantius Firmianus, not the least among theologians. Those who neglect the goods of the soul and desire those of the body, he says, spend their lives in shadows and death.[2] This statement from our Cicero's work *On Duties* you have also respected: For we are all drawn and led to the desire for knowledge and science, in which we think it fine to excel, but [consider it] shameful and base to falter, wander, be deceived and ignorant.[3] This does not escape that shrewd orator Quintilian in his *Oratoria institutio*: For just as birds are born for flight, horses for the race, wild beasts for savagery, so to us is distinctive a certain vitality and swiftness of mind.[4] All these maxims you have gathered to your breast always and guarded diligently. This being so, you must be judged the equal of those most excellent learned women of whom in antiquity there was no small multitude. Such were Aspasia,[5] Cornelia, Scipio's daughter,[6] Elphe,[7] and others of whom this is not the place to speak. Indeed you, who for some considerable time have excelled in studies, know this far better than I. I cannot express in words how much I admire you; [whatever I say] falls short of what is in my mind. And please believe that there is nothing which contributes to the sum of your merit which, I promise, I shall not willingly undertake with all my strength to perform.

IO

*Of the Equal or Unequal Sin of Adam and Eve:*
*An honorable disputation between the illustrious lord*
*Ludovico Foscarini, Venetian doctor of arts and both*
*laws, and the noble and learned and divine lady Isotta*
*Nogarola of Verona, regarding this judgment of*
*Aurelius Augustine: They sinned unequally according to*
*sex, but equally according to pride.*[1]

## Introduction

The dialogue translated below is one of the most significant works by a woman humanist penned during the Quattrocento. The dialogue, on the relative guilt of Adam and Eve, is a discussion between Ludovico Foscarini, a Venetian nobleman, and Isotta Nogarola, composed by Isotta (with Ludovico's encouragement) from letters exchanged between them.[2]

Ludovico Foscarini was a well-known figure in Venetian culture, a diplomat, lawyer and humanist.[3] Between 1451 and 1453 he and Isotta developed a close friendship through their correspondence. Although only one of her letters to him survives (apart from these related to the Adam and Eve debate), a number of his to her exist, and they reveal a relationship as passionate as that of two lovers. More than anyone else, he lifted—for a time—her veil of isolation and allowed her to enter into the world of male culture more than she had done before or was to do afterwards. When she received a proposal of marriage she aked his advice; he told her in strong terms to maintain her present course—advice which she followed. She, in turn, suggested to him the possibility of giving up his life as a diplomat and entering a religious retreat similar to hers, but in two letters responding to her he suggested that she had chosen the nobler path, while he had chosen to serve Caesar. Thus it must remain.

Given the nature of the relationship between them, it is not surprising that in their epistolary discussion of the relative responsibility of Adam and Eve for the fall and its consequences, they engaged in a veritable battle of the sexes, with Isotta defending Eve and Ludovico Adam.

Ludovico opens the debate by stating but not defending his position that Eve was more guilty because she received a harsher punishment, was motivated by pride, and was the cause of Adam's sin (not he of hers). Isotta responds that Eve could not be more guilty than Adam because Eve was weaker, lacking in constancy. It was because of her weakness (rather than her pride) that she ate of the fruit of the tree. Moreover, even at the beginning, when God placed the two in Eden, he made Adam responsible, telling him (not them) not to eat of the fruit of the tree of knowledge. Finally, Isotta contends, Eve was not given a harsher punishment, for while she was told that she would deliver children in pain, Adam was punished with labor and death.

Ludovico responds that Eve did not sin from ignorance or, if she did, is still responsible for her sin. If she was inconstant, she is responsible for that as well. Her sin was not her frailty but her pride, which was overweening. Moreover, Adam's punishment was not more severe than Eve's, for Eve became subject to labor and death as much as Adam did, in addition to which she also was punished with bearing children in pain.

So much for the refutation of Isotta's arguments. Turning to his own position, Ludovico contends that Eve sinned more greatly because it was on her account that Adam sinned. She set the example for Adam and he, out of his love for her, followed it.

To this Isotta responds that Eve's ignorance was not crass or affected but implanted by God, and ignorance of this kind certainly excuses sin. Her inconstancy, then, derives from the fact that she was created an imperfect creature to begin with. Adam, on the other hand, was created perfect. It was to Adam that God gave dominion over the earth. Even Adam's body was more perfect, since God created Adam's body himself, but he created Eve's body from Adam's.

Still further, even if Eve sinned out of pride (the desire to know good and evil), her sin was less than Adam's, who transgressed a divine commandment. So slight was Eve's sin, in fact, that no reference was made to her redemption. Her crime was not great enough to require redemption. Thus if man merited redemption, woman all the more so did, because her sin was less. Nor can Eve's case be compared with that of the fallen angels, who cannot plead Eve's weakness of nature.

That Adam's sin was greater than Eve's can be proved, Isotta continues, by the fact that it required Christ's suffering to redeem it. Neither can it be argued that Eve is more guilty because of her example—that she caused Adam to sin. For Eve was inferior to Adam. Therefore, Eve could not constrain Adam's free will. If he had free will, he is more guilty; and if he did not, it was God who took it from him, not Eve. Moreover, since Eve was weaker than Adam, she sinned less in following the serpent than Adam did in following her. The fact that Eve sinned before Adam (and hence for a longer time) is also of no consequence, since Eve was weaker; it was not the case of sin among equals. Finally, Eve's example does not make her more guilty. The Jews, who were not ignorant of God's laws, prophets and the signs concerning Christ, were condemned more harshly than Pilate, who was.

Ludovico responds that Eve's inconstancy was not innate but rather a moral choice. And even if Eve were inferior to Adam, nonetheless God implanted reason in her sufficient for the health of her soul. If she were created to console Adam she failed and, instead, brought him sorrow. The argument that Adam broke a divine commandment does not acquit Eve, since she did not keep the commandment either. Finally, regarding the discussion of Eve's example, Ludovico avers that the female sex in general is deceitful. His words close the debate.

Structurally, the arguments just recounted are of three kinds. First, Isotta argues Eve's weakness to excuse her from responsibility both for her own sin and for that of Adam, while Ludovico argues Eve's pride and willful (moral) choice to condemn her both for her own sin and for Adam's. Second, Isotta argues the limited character of Eve's sin to minimize its harmfulness and the unlimited character of Adam's sin (against a divine commandment) to maximize its seriousness (it required Christ to redeem it), while Ludovico argues that both disobeyed a divine commandment and that Eve's was never redeemed. Finally, Isotta argues that Eve's punishment was less than Adam's (painful childbirth as opposed to labor and death), while Ludovico argues that it was greater (labor and death *and* painful childbirth).

Who won the debate? Ingenuity and imagination aside (in which Isotta holds the upper hand), Ludovico clearly won, because Isotta's defense is based essentially on a confession of Eve's weakness and inferiority to Adam. Isotta had so thoroughly accepted her culture's evaluation of the worth of women that she could not defend her sex without at the same time undermining its dignity.

This translation is based on the Latin text published by Abel in Nogarola, *Opera*, 2:187–216.

## *Text*

LUDOVICO BEGINS: If it is in any way possible to measure the gravity of human sinfulness, then we should see Eve's sin as more to be condemned than Adam's [for three reasons]. [First], she was assigned by a just judge to a harsher punishment than was Adam. [Second], she believed that she was made more like God, and that is in the category of unforgiveable sins against the Holy Spirit. [Third], she suggested and was the cause of Adam's sin – not he of hers; and although it is a poor excuse to sin because of a friend, nevertheless none was more tolerable than the one by which Adam was enticed.

ISOTTA: But I see things – since you move me to reply – from quite another and contrary viewpoint. For where there is less intellect and less constancy, there there is less sin; and Eve [lacked sense and constancy] and therefore sinned less. Knowing [her weakness] that crafty serpent began by tempting the woman, thinking the man perhaps invulnerable because of his constancy. [For it says in] *Sentences* 2:[4] Standing in the woman's presence, the ancient foe did not boldly persuade, but approached her with a question: "Why did God bid you not to eat of the tree of paradise?" She responded: "Lest perhaps we die." But seeing that she doubted the words of the Lord, the devil said: "You shall not die," but "you will be like God, knowing good and evil."[5]

[Adam must also be judged more guilty than Eve, secondly] because of his greater contempt for the command. For in Genesis 2 it appears that the Lord commanded Adam, not Eve, where it says: "The Lord God took the man and placed him in the paradise of Eden to till it and to keep it," (and it does not say, "that they might care for and protect it") ". . . and the Lord God commanded the man" (and not "them"): "From every tree of the garden you may eat" (and not "you" [in the plural sense]), and, [referring to the forbidden tree], "for the day you eat of it, you must die," [again, using the singular form of "you"].[6] [God directed his command to Adam alone] because he esteemed the man more highly than the woman.

Moreover, the woman did not [eat from the forbidden tree] because she believed that she was made more like God, but rather because she was weak and [inclined to indulge in] pleasure. Thus: "Now the woman saw that the tree was good for food, pleasing to the eyes, and desirable for the knowledge it would give. She took of its fruit and ate it, and also gave some to her husband and he ate,"[7] and it does not say [that she did so] in order to be like God. And if Adam had not eaten, her sin would have had no consequences. For it does not say: "If Eve had not sinned Christ would not have been made incarnate," but "If Adam had not sinned."[8] Hence the woman, but only because she had been first deceived by the serpent's evil persuasion, did indulge in the delights of paradise; but she would have harmed only herself and in no way endangered human posterity if the consent of the first-born man had not been offered. Therefore Eve was no danger to posterity but [only] to herself; but the man Adam spread the infection of sin to himself and to all future generations. Thus Adam, being the author of all humans yet to be born, was also the first cause of their perdition. For this reason the healing of humankind was celebrated first in the man and then in the woman, just as [according to Jewish tradition], after an unclean spirit has been expelled from a man, as it springs forth from the synagogue, the woman is purged [as well].

Moreover, that Eve was condemned by a just judge to a harsher punishment is evidently false, for God said to the woman: "I will make great your distress in childbearing; in pain shall you bring forth children; for your husband shall be your longing, though he have dominion over you."[9] But to Adam he said: "Because you have listened to your wife and have eaten of the tree of which I have commanded you not to eat" (notice that God appears to have admonished Adam alone [using the singular form of "you"] and not Eve) "Cursed be the ground because of you; in toil shall you eat of it all the days of your life; thorns and thistles shall it bring forth to you, and you shall eat the plants of the field. In the sweat of your brow you shall eat bread, till you return to the ground, since out of it you were taken; for dust you are and unto dust you shall return."[10] Notice that Adam's punishment appears harsher than Eve's; for God said to Adam: "to dust you shall return," and not to Eve, and death is the most terrible punishment that could be assigned. Therefore it is established that Adam's punishment was greater than Eve's.

I have written this because you wished me to. Yet I have done so fearfully, since this is not a woman's task. But you are kind, and if you find any part of my writing clumsy you will correct it.

LUDOVICO: You defend the cause of Eve most subtly, and indeed defend it so [well] that, if I had not been born a man, you would have made me your champion. But sticking fast to the truth, which is attached by very strong roots, I have set out [here] to assault your fortress with your own weapons. I shall begin by attacking its foundations, which can be destroyed by the testimony of Sacred Scripture, so that there will be no lack of material for my refutation.

Eve sinned from ignorance and inconstancy, from which you conclude that she sinned less seriously. [But] ignorance—especially of those things which we are obligated to know—does not excuse us. For it is written: "If anyone ignores this, he shall be ignored."[11] The eyes which guilt makes blind punishment opens. He who has been foolish in guilt will be wise in punishment, especially when the sinner's mistake occurs through negligence. For the woman's ignorance, born of arrogance, does not excuse her, in the same way that Aristotle and the [lawyers], who teach a true philosophy, find the drunk and ignorant deserving of a double punishment.[12] Nor do I understand how in the world you, so many ages distant from Eve, fault her intellect, when her knowledge, divinely created by the highest craftsman of all things, daunted that clever serpent lurking in paradise. For, as you write, he was not bold enough to attempt to persuade her but approached her with a question.

But the acts due to inconstancy are even more blameworthy [than those due to ignorance]. For to the same degree that the acts issuing from a solid and constant mental attitude are more worthy and distinct from the preceding ones, so should those issuing from inconstancy be punished more severely, since inconstancy is an evil in itself and when paired with an evil sin makes the sin worse.

Nor is Adam's companion excused because Adam was appointed to protect her, [contrary to your contention that] thieves who have been trustingly employed by a householder are not punished with the most severe punishment like strangers or those in whom no confidence has been placed. Also, the woman's frailty was not the cause of sin, as you write, but her pride, since the demon promised her knowledge, which leads to arrogance and inflates [with pride], according to the apostle.[13] For it says in Ecclesiasticus: "Pride was the beginning of every sin."[14] And though the other women followed, yet she was the first since, when man existed in a state of innocence, the flesh was obedient to him and [did not struggle] against reason. The first impulse [of sin], therefore, was an inordinate appetite for seeking that which was not suited to its own nature, as Augustine wrote to Orosius: "Swollen by pride, man obeyed the serpent's persuasion and disdained God's commands."[15] For the adversary said to Eve: "Your eyes will be opened and you will be like God, knowing good and evil."[16] Nor would the woman have believed the demon's persuasive words, as Augustine says [in his commentary] on Genesis, unless a love of her own power had overcome her, which [love is] a stream sprung from the well of pride.[17] [I shall continue to follow Augustine in his view that at the moment] when Eve desired to capture divinity, she lost happiness. And those words: "If Adam had not sinned, etc." confirm me in my view. For Eve sinned perhaps in such a way that, just as the demons did not merit redemption, neither perhaps did she. I speak only in jest, but Adam's sin was fortunate, since it warranted such a redeemer.[18]

And lest I finally stray too far from what you have written, [I shall turn to your argument that Adam's punishment was more severe than Eve's and his sin, accordingly, greater. But] the woman suffers all the penalties [inflicted on] the man, and since her sorrows are greater than his, not only is she doomed to death, condemned to eat at the cost of sweat, denied by the cherubim and flaming swords entry to paradise, but in addition to all these things which are common [to both], she alone must give birth in pain and be subjected to her husband. [Her punishment is thus harsher than Adam's, as her sin is greater].

But because in such a matter it is not sufficient to have refuted your arguments without also putting forward my own, [I shall do so now]. Eve believed that she was made similar to God and, out of envy, desired that which wounds the Holy Spirit. Moreover, she must bear responsibility for every fault of Adam because, as Aristotle testifies, the cause of a cause is the cause of that which is caused.[19] Indeed, every prior cause influences an outcome more than a secondary cause, and the principle of any genus, according to the same Aristotle, is seen as its greatest [component]. In fact, [it] is considered to be more than half the whole.[20] And in the *Posterior Analytics* he writes: "That on account of which any thing exists is that thing and more greatly so."[21] Now [since] Adam sinned on account of Eve, it follows that Eve sinned much more than Adam. Similarly, just as it is better to treat others well than to be well-treated, so it is worse to persuade another to evil than to be persuaded to evil. For he sins less who sins by another's example, inasmuch as what is done by example can be said to be done according to a kind of law, [and thus justly]. For this reason it is commonly said that "the sins that many commit are [without fault]." [Thus Eve, who persuaded her husband to commit an evil act, sinned more greatly than Adam, who merely consented to her example]. And if Adam and Eve both had thought that they were worthy of the same glory, Eve, who was inferior [by nature], more greatly departed from the mean, and consequently sinned more greatly. Moreover, as a beloved companion she could deceive her husband [vulnerable to her persuasion because of his love for her] more easily than the shameful serpent could deceive the woman. And she persevered longer [in sin] than Adam, because she began first, and offenses are that much more serious (according to Gregory's decree) in relation to the length of time they hold the unhappy soul in bondage.[22] Finally, to bring my discourse to a close, Eve was the cause and the example of sin, and Gregory greatly increases the guilt in the case of the example.[23] And Christ, who could not err, condemned more severely the pretext of the ignorant Jews, because it came first, than he did the sentence of the learned Pilate, when he said: "They who have betrayed me to you have greater sin, etc."[24] All who wish to be called Christians have always agreed with this judgment, and you, above all most Christian, will approve and defend it. Farewell, and do not fear, but dare to do much, because you have excellently understood so much and write so learnedly.

ISOTTA: I had decided that I would not enter further into a contest with you because, as you say, you assault my fortress with my own weapons. [The propositions] you have presented me were so perfectly and diligently defended that it would be difficult not merely for me, but for the most learned men, to oppose them. But since I recognize that this contest is useful for me, I have decided to obey your honest wish. Even though I know I struggle in vain, yet I will earn the highest praise if I am defeated by so mighty a man as you.

Eve sinned out of ignorance and inconstancy, and hence you contend that she sinned more gravely, because the ignorance of those things which we are obligated to know does not excuse us, since it is written: "He who does not know will not be known." I would concede your point if that ignorance were crude or affected. But Eve's ignorance was implanted by nature, of which nature God himself is the author and founder. In many people it is seen that he who knows less sins less, like a boy who sins less than an old man or a peasant less than a noble. Such a person does not need to know explicitly what is required for salvation, but implicitly, because [for him] faith alone suffices. The question of inconstancy proceeds similarly. For when it is said that the acts which proceed from inconstancy are more blameworthy, [that kind of] inconstancy is understood which is not innate but the product of character and sins.

The same is true of imperfection. For when gifts increase, greater responsibility is imposed. When God created man, from the beginning he created him perfect, and the powers of his soul perfect, and gave him a greater understanding and knowledge of truth as well as a greater depth of wisdom. Thus it was that the Lord led to Adam all the animals of the earth and the birds of heaven, so that Adam could call them by their names. For God said: "Let us make mankind in our image and likeness, and let them have dominion over the fish of the sea, and the birds of the air, the cattle, over all the wild animals and every creature that crawls on the earth,"[25] making clear his own perfection. But of the woman he said: "It is not good that the man is alone; I will make him a helper like himself."[26] And since consolation and joy are required for happiness, and since no one can have solace and joy when alone, it appears that God created woman for man's consolation. For the good spreads itself, and the greater it is the more it shares itself. Therefore, it appears that Adam's sin was greater than Eve's. [As] Ambrose [says]: "In him to whom a more indulgent liberality has been shown is insolence more inexcusable."[27]

"But Adam's companion," [you argue], "is not excused because Adam was appointed to protect her, because thieves who have been trustingly employed by a householder are not punished with the most severe punishment like strangers or those in whom the householder placed no confidence." This is true, however, in temporal law, but not in divine law, for divine justice proceeds differently from temporal justice in punishing [sin].

[You argue further that] "the fragility of the woman was not the cause of sin, but rather her inordinate appetite for seeking that which was not suited to her nature," which [appetite] is the product, as you write, of pride. Yet it is clearly less a sin to desire the knowledge of good and evil than to transgress against a divine commandment, since the desire for knowledge is a natural thing, and all men by nature desire to know.[28] And even if the first impulse [of sin] were this inordinate appetite, which cannot be without sin, yet it is more tolerable than the sin of transgression, for the observance of the commandments is the road which leads to the country of salvation. [It is written]: "But if thou wilt enter into life, keep the commandments;"[29] and likewise: "What shall I do to gain eternal life? Keep the commandments."[30] And transgression is particularly born of pride, because pride is nothing other than rebellion against divine rule, exalting oneself above what is permitted according to divine rule, by disdaining the will of God and displacing it with one's own. Thus Augustine [writes] in *On Nature and Grace*: "Sin is the will to pursue or retain what justice forbids, that is, to deny what God wishes."[31] Ambrose agrees with him in his *On Paradise*: "Sin is the transgression against divine law and disobedience to the heavenly commandments."[32] Behold! See that the transgression against and disobedience to the heavenly commandments is the greatest sin, whereas you have thus defined sin: "Sin is the inordinate desire to know." Thus clearly the sin of transgression against a command is greater than [the sin of] desiring the knowledge of good and evil. So even if inordinate desire be a sin, as with Eve, yet she did not desire to be like God in power but only in the knowledge of good and evil, which by nature she was actually inclined to desire.

[Next, as to your statement] that those words, "if Adam had not sinned," confirm you in your view [of Eve's damnability], since Eve may have so sinned that, like the demons, she did not merit redemption, I reply that she also was redeemed with Adam, because [she was] "bone of my bone and flesh of my flesh."[33] And if it seems that God did not redeem her, this was undoubtedly because God held her sin as negligible. For if man deserved redemption, the woman deserved it much more because of the slightness of the crime. For the angel cannot be excused by ignorance as can the woman. For the angel understands without investigation or discussion and has an intellect more in the likeness of God's — to which it seems Eve desired to be similar — than does man. Hence the angel is called intellectual and the man rational. Thus where the woman sinned from her desire for knowledge, the angel sinned from a desire for power. While knowledge of an appearance in some small way can be partaken of by the creature, in no way can it partake in the power of God and of the soul of Christ. Moreover, the woman in sinning thought she would receive mercy, believing certainly that she was committing a sin, but not one so great as to warrant God's inflicting such a sentence and punishment. But the angel did not think [of mercy]. Hence Gregory [says in the] fourth book of the *Moralia*: "The first parents were needed for this, that the sin which they committed by transgressing they might purge by confessing."[34] But that persuasive serpent was never punished for his sin, for he was never to be re-called to grace. Thus, in sum, Eve clearly merited redemption more than the angels.

[As to your argument] that the woman also suffers all the penalties inflicted on the man, and beyond those which are common [to both] she alone gives birth in sorrow and has been subjected to man, this also reinforces my earlier point. As I said, the good spreads itself, and the greater it is the more it shares itself. So also evil, the greater it is the more it shares itself, and the more it shares itself the more harmful it is, and the more harmful it is the greater it is. Furthermore, the severity of the punishment is proportional to the gravity of the sin. Hence Christ chose to die on the cross, though this was the most shameful and horrible kind of death, and on the cross he endured in general every kind of suffering by type. Hence Isidore writes concerning the Trinity: "The only-born Son of God in executing the sacrament of his death, in himself bears witness that he consummated every kind of suffering when, with lowered head, he gave up his spirit."[35] The reason was that the punishment had to cor-respond to the guilt. Adam took the fruit of the forbidden tree; Christ suf-fered on the tree and so made satisfaction [for Adam's sin]. [As] Augustine [writes]: "Adam disdained God's command" (and he does not say Eve) "accept-ing the fruit from the tree, but whatever Adam lost Christ restored."[36] [For Christ paid the penalty for sin he had not committed, as it says in] Psalm 64: "For what I have not taken, then I atoned."[37] Therefore, Adam's sin was the greatest [possible], because the punishment corresponding to his fault was the greatest [possible] and was general in all men. [As the] apostle [says]: "All sinned in Adam."[38]

"Eve," [you say], "must bear responsibility for every fault of Adam because, as Aristotle shows, whatever is the cause of the cause is the cause of the thing caused." This is true in the case of things which are, as you know better [than I], in themselves the causes of other things, which is the case for the first cause, the first principle, and "that on account of which anything is what it is." But clearly this was not the case with Eve, because Adam either had free will or he did not. If he did not have it, he did not sin; if he had it, then Eve forced the sin [upon him], which is impossible. For as Bernard says: "Free will, because of its inborn nobility, is forced by no necessity,"[39] not even by God, because if that were the case it would be to concede that two contradictories are true at the same time. God cannot do, therefore, what would cause an act proceeding from free will and remaining free to be not free but coerced. [As] Augustine [writes in his commentary] on Genesis: "God cannot act against that nature which he created with a good will."[40] God could himself, however, remove that condition of liberty from any person and bestow some other condition on him. In the same way fire cannot, while it remains fire, not burn, unless its nature is changed and suspended for a time by divine force. No other creature, such as a good angel or devil can do this, since they are less than God; much less a woman, since she is less perfect and weaker than they. Augustine clarifies this principle [of God's supremacy] saying: "Above our mind is nothing besides God, nor is there anything intermediary between God and our mind."[41] Yet only something which is superior to something else can coerce it; but Eve was inferior to Adam, therefore she was not herself the cause of sin. [In] Ecclesiasticus 15 [it says]: "God from the beginning created man and placed him in the palm of his counsel and made clear his commandments and precepts. If you wish to preserve the commandments, they will preserve you and create in you pleasing faith."[42] Thus Adam appeared to accuse God rather than excuse himself when he said: "The woman you placed at my side gave me fruit from the tree and I ate it."[43]

[Next you argue] that the beloved companion could have more easily deceived the man than the shameful serpent the woman. To this I reply that Eve, weak and ignorant by nature, sinned much less by assenting to that astute serpent, who was called "wise," than Adam — created by God with perfect knowledge and understanding — in listening to the persuasive words and voice of the imperfect woman.

[Further, you say] that Eve persevered in her sin a longer time and therefore sinned more, because crimes are that much more serious according to the length of time they hold the unhappy soul in bondage. This is no doubt true, when two sins are equal, and in the same person or in two similar persons. But Adam and Eve were not equals, because Adam was a perfect animal and Eve imperfect and ignorant. [Therefore, their sins were not comparable, and Eve, who persevered longer in sin, was not on that account more guilty than Adam].

Finally, if I may quote you: "The woman was the example and the cause of sin, and Gregory emphatically extends the burden of guilt to [the person who provided] an example, and Christ condemned the cause of the ignorant Jews, because it was first, more than the learned Pilate's sentence when he said: 'Therefore he who betrayed me to you has greater sin.' " I reply that Christ did not condemn the cause of the ignorant Jews because it was first, but because it was vicious and devilish due to their native malice and obstinacy. For they did not sin from ignorance. The gentile Pilate was more ignorant about these things than the Jews, who had the law and the prophets and read them and daily saw signs concerning [Christ]. For John 15 says: "If I had not come and spoken to them, they would have no sin. But now they have no excuse for their sin."[44] Thus they themselves said: "What are we doing? for this man is working signs."[45] And: "Art thou the Christ, the Son of the Blessed One?"[46] For the [Jewish] people was special to God, and Christ himself [said]: "I was not sent except to the lost sheep of the house of Israel. It is not fair to take the children's bread and cast it to the dogs."[47] Therefore the Jews sinned more, because Jesus loved them more.

Let these words be enough from me, an unarmed and poor little woman.

LUDOVICO: So divinely have you encompassed the whole of this problem that I could believe your words were drawn not from the fonts of philosophy and theology but from heaven. Hence they are worthy of praise rather than contradiction. Yet, lest you be cheated of the utility [you say you have begun to receive from this debate], attend to these brief arguments which can be posed for the opposite view, that you may sow the honey-sweet seeds of paradise which will delight readers and surround you with glory.

Eve's ignorance was very base, because she chose to put faith in a demon rather than in the creator. This ignorance actually is due to her sin, as sacred writings attest, and certainly does not excuse her sin. Indeed, if the truth be plainly told, it was extreme stupidity not to remain within the boundaries which the excellent God had set for her, [but] to fall prey to vain hope and lose what she had had and what she aspired to.

The issues which you have cleverly joined I shall not divide. The inconstancy of Eve which has been condemned was not an inconstancy of nature but of habit. For those qualities which are in us by nature we are neither praised nor blamed, according to the judgment of the wisest philosophers. Actually, the woman's nature was excellent and concordant with reason, genus and time. For just as teeth were given to wild beasts, horns to oxen, feathers to birds for their survival, to the woman mental capacity was given sufficient for the preservation and pursuit of the health of her soul.

If [as you say] Eve was naturally created to aid, perfect, console and gladden man, she conducted herself contrary to the laws [of her nature], providing him with toil, imperfection, sadness and sorrow, which the holy decrees had ordained would be serious crimes. And human laws, too, ordered through long ages by the minds of great men, by sure reasoning have established that the seizure of someone else's goods merits the more serious punishment the more it injures the owner.

Your argument about [Adam's] transgression of God's commandments does not acquit Eve [of responsibility], because neither did she keep them. As to your distinction between the sin of the angel and of man, [by means of which you argue that Eve's sin was less serious than that of the rebellious angels, and thus redeemable], that is a huge issue, and though it provides worthy food for your brilliant mind, it is too abundant to consider in this brief space. And how you can consider it to be concordant with the principle of the highest God's goodness that greater punishments are poured out upon those who have sinned less [−for you argue that the evil consequences of Adam's sin, when diffused to Eve, whose being had derived from his, were intensified−] I cannot understand.

You push too far Aristotle's views on first causes. [You agree that] every cause of a cause is a cause of the thing caused, [but argue that since Adam had free will his act could not have been caused by Eve]. But since Adam had free will, I do not consider him free from obligation to sin, and even though I have assigned Adam's whole fault in some degree to Eve, yet [I do not contend] that Adam's sin was entirely and in every way caused by Eve.

I agree [with what you say] concerning free will and the [essential] goodness of [human] nature.

As to the ease of the man's consent to the woman's words, [which you see as indicating his sinful weakness], I want, since I am writing to you, to pass by in silence the matter of the deceitfulness of the [female] sex. But this ancient proverb states: "There is no plague more deadly than an intimate enemy."[48] The first mother kindled a great fire, which to our ruin has not yet been extinguished.[49] This demonstrates the extreme seriousness of her sin. For just as those sicknesses of the body are more serious which are less curable, so the [diseases] of the soul [which Eve brought upon us are serious indeed].

Though I have spoken, you may not hear. You may spurn and disdain [my words because of] Augustine's conclusion that they were equally guilty: "The principle of how much longer, etc." Let us read the history of the passion and the dreams of the wife, the words of Pilate, the washing of hands, the avoidance of judgment, and we shall confess that he understood better than the Jews that the sentence was unjust. These things make it quite clear that the force of my arguments has not been weakened.

I have explained my views with these few words, both because I was ordered not to exceed the paper [you] sent me, and because I speak to you who are most learned. For I do not wish to be a guide on such a road to you for whom, because of your great goodness, all things stand open in the brightest light. I, indeed—a single man and a mere mortal, as it were, a reflection of the celestial life—have only pointed a finger, so to speak, in the direction of the sources. And although others may find that my writings suffer from the defect of obscurity, if you, most brilliant, accept them and join them to what you and I have already written, our views will become very evident and clear, and will shine amid the shadows. And if what I have written is clumsy, by your skill you will make it worthy of your mind, virtue, and glory. For you march forward to new battles to the sound of sacred eloquence (as do soldiers to the clamor of trumpets), always more learned and more ready. And you march forward against me, who has applied the whole sum of my thinking to my reading, all at the same time, and to my writing, that I might present my case and defend myself against yours, although the many storms and floods of my obligations toss me about at whim. Farewell.

## II

### Oration of Cassandra Fedele, Maiden of Venice, in the University of Padua, for Bertucio Lamberto, Canon of Concordia, Receiving the Honors of the Liberal Arts

### Introduction

In 1487, when Cassandra delivered this oration, she was twenty-two years old and culminating her classical education. It was one of the crowning achievements of her studies, and well it might have been, for it is one of the earliest precedents for women's involvement in university life. There is not a little irony in the fact that Cassandra was invited to address a body of scholars among whom she was not allowed to study.[1] In addition to this oration, Cassandra delivered several others during the same period.

Although Cassandra says that a good education is one which tends toward religion and piety, there is not one religious reference in this address. All her citations are from classical Greek and Roman sources, as the notes indicate. The content of the oration places it in the genre of moral philosophy. All her references to the advantages of studying philosophy suggest that the purpose of philosophical study is to enhance one's resources for living well.

Bertucio Lamberto, in whose honor the speech is delivered, is unknown to us from other sources. [2]

This translation is based on the Latin text in *Cassandra Fidelis epistolae et orationes*, ed. Tomasini, pp. 193–201. [2a]

## *Text*

I F I WERE PERMITTED TO BE AFRAID as I bravely start to speak, honorable fathers, governors of the university, and most illustrious gentlemen, then faced with these ranks of learned men I would falter, bow and bend. But it behooves me, I know, to be brave. And so I shall contain my timidity — although I know it might seem to many of you audacious that I, a virgin too young to be learned, ignoring my sex and exceeding my talent, should propose to speak before such a body of learned men, and especially in this city where today (as once in Athens) the study of the liberal arts flourishes. However, the bond of duty and blood which joins me to Bertucio has forced me to undertake this task against my will, since I prefer to be called too bold rather than, by shirking my duty to a relative to whom I owe loyalty, diligent service and respect, to be too hard. There are other considerations which almost discouraged me from beginning; now, however, they in particular incite and impel me to undertake this task. So relying on your singular kindness and your rare courtesy, I dare to advance to speak. I knew that your kindness would absolve me if, in the course of my speech, I said something inelegant or unlearned. Indeed, I believe that you are endowed not only with this virtue but all others. Of these I would gladly speak if I were not afraid that needlessly to detain you with a long oration would be wearisome and unwise and that it would be exceedingly rash to judge that I could praise your virtues as much as I ought. So I will not assume that task, though I will touch on the matter, since it would be more difficult for me to end your praises than to begin them. So with this encouragement, I shall set my sails on a new course. I must speak of my [cousin], or appear to shirk my duty. I shall speak briefly.

I have chosen as the subject of my praise the threefold tradition of Cicero, Plato, and the Peripatetics, who believed that men derived true honor from the goods of the soul, the goods of the body, and from those goods which some prominent philosophers ascribed to fortune. [3] Therefore, I beseech you, illustrious gentlemen, to pay close attention, although I know that you expect no profound insights from me. Lest you think that I speak ostentatiously (which I am striving particularly not to do), I shall use humble, everyday words, which

I am sure will please you. However brilliant one's origin, it is granted highest praise, as you know, only when the record of one's virtues achieves the level of one's nobility. These virtues alone add glory to one's family name and make people truly noble and truly famous. For what is the point of praising my relative's [Bertucio's] origin more than his character and learning, his quick, versatile, and receptive disposition, his tenacious memory or his remarkable love of the good arts? It would mean little, indeed, to have been born among the Venetians in the most celebrated marketplace of the whole world, if there were not added [to that merit] an education inferior to none with respect to religion and piety. And he has many friends, many admirers, many supporters of his glory. [Yet] the more he is praised, the less is he arrogant and overbearing. Look upon his skillfulness and dignity of form: how innocently and piously he has spent his youth is clearly evident. A youth more obedient to his parents does not exist, nor ever did. In all, to sum up, to that degree that he seems to be green in age, he is ripe, you will discover, in virtue. All this is obvious, or I would not have dared to mention it before so great an assembly. But now I shall turn to more serious matters.

Riches, bodily strength, and other such things pass away in a brief time. Deeds of genius, by contrast, are immortal, as is the soul, while goods of the body and of fortune [are snatched away]: the end is like the beginning. Neither money nor, I believe, magnificent houses nor wealth nor other pleasures of that kind which many pursue, should be counted as good things. Never, indeed, is such hungry craving satisfied, never filled. For who can deny that our weak and changeable flesh is fleeting? Yet where now is magnificent Thebes, adorned with such a luxuriance of buildings?[4] Where is the splendor of the Persians and their Cyrus?[5] Where is Darius?[6] Where are the Macedonians with their kings Philip and Alexander?[7] Where are the Spartans with their Lycurgus?[8] Where is the strength of invincible Hercules?[9] It was not beauty preserved which made Spurina famous, but beauty ruined, [his] face [scarred] by wounds for the sake of chastity.[10] Who can possess these [fleeting goods] securely? Necessity appoints [their fate] equally to the greatest and the least. Was not even Croesus, king of the Lydians, deprived of an immense treasure of wealth and riches by Cyrus?[11] Then a cheap little woman robbed Cyrus in turn of both kingdom and life.[12] And Xerxes, who roared across land and sea with a great fleet of ships, fled back to his kingdom, content with the wood of one little ship, his whole army lost.[13] I could go on and on. Where is Rome, that tamer of barbarians and ruler of the Greeks? Clearly, all these things have withered away. Terrible death attends all fleeting things. But those things which are produced by virtue and intelligence are useful to those who follow.

In the same way now here our Bertucio, having with keen mind and excellent memory devoted all his attention and studies to eloquence from his earliest

years, now flourishes, [possessed of a] fluency and singular grace in speech.
These very studies also add much honor and ornament to the advantages of
fortune and of the body. For it is in speech that men excel beasts. What is
so uncultivated, so unpolished, so unintelligible, so base, that it cannot be set
aglow and, so to speak, ennobled by a carefully wrought oration? What is
more praiseworthy than eloquence, more outstanding, or more lovely, whether
[greeted] by the admiration of listeners or the hope of those in need or the
thanks of those who have been defended? Nothing, moreover, is so incredible
or difficult that it cannot become acceptable and easy through speaking. And
how much more humane, praiseworthy and noble do those states and princes
become who support and cultivate these studies! Certainly for this reason this
part of philosophy has laid claim for itself to the sweet name of "humanity,"
since those who are rough by nature become by these studies more civil and
mild-mannered. But I am here to praise the youth [Bertucio], pursuing the
study of philosophy, which [branch of] knowledge has always been thought
divine among the wisest men, and rightly so. For the other disciplines deal
with matters related to man; this one teaches clearly what man himself is, what
he must strive for, what he must flee. There is no understanding of life, no
outstanding principle, and, finally, nothing which pertains to living well and
happily, which does not result from the study of philosophy. Has anyone ever
plunged into error who was imbued with philosophy? These studies refine the
mind, intensify and strengthen the force of reason. The minds of men who
have lapsed into error are set straight by this rudder. For this reason Stratonicus
rightly calls philosophy the true security.[14] Our minds striving, by means of
philosophy, we are able to discover truth and to know hidden things; she is
the perfect craftsman and teacher of happiness. For what is more fruitfully
useful? What [contributes] more to dignity, what more happily to righteous
pleasure, or more aptly to the glory of cities than the branches of philosophy?
For this reason Plato, a man almost divine, wrote that republics are blessed
when their administrators have been trained in philosophy, or when men trained
in philosophy have undertaken to administer them.[15]

Various inventors of this holy discipline of wisdom are reported.[16] The
Africans cite Atlas; The Thracians cite Orpheus or Zamolxis; the Thebans cite
Linus; the Egyptians Vulcan; the Gauls their Druids; others cite other men
who were the first to lay down the foundations of philosophy or to build on
them to some extent. Philosophy, whether its origin is traced to Zoroaster,
prince of the Magi, or to the Gymnosophists of the Persians and Chaldaeans,
is divided into rational, moral, and natural philosophy.

It is not easy to describe the careful diligence with which [Bertucio] has spent
a lifetime in these studies. As much time as others are accustomed to devote
to celebrating festive days, to the pleasures of the spirit, to the repose of the

body, so much time has he devoted to the cultivation of these studies. Now indeed the reward, the dignity, he has earned by means of these labors and vigils, I need not mention to you, most worthy men, since you, in your wisdom, have judged that he should be awarded the insignia of philosophy; although it must not be doubted that he will attain still higher rewards in the future.

I would speak at greater length if I did not know that Johannes Regius, whom you heard a little while ago, had spoken with greater elegance.[17] Since that is so, distinguished gentlemen, lest by a longer speech I turn your joy to boredom, I shall pass over the rest. I attend instead to my particular duty, to extend thanks particularly to you, illustrious magistrates of this city, and to you, excellent fathers and distinguished men, because you have deigned to lend your welcome presence in a distinguished assembly to honor my relative. For no one is so ungrateful or insensitive or crude that he would neglect to praise you for this recent favor. But, to tell the truth, there could hardly be an orator so consummate and with such discerning judgment who could—I do not say recount all your merits (for this cannot be done)—but even touch lightly upon them. Happy, therefore, are you, Cassandra, that you happened to be born into these times! Happy this age and this excellent city of Padua, overbrimming with so many learned men. Now let everyone cease, cease, I say, to marvel at the ancients! The highest and greatest God has wished the studies of all peoples to flourish in this place, and to be commended and consecrated to eternity. For age will exhaust and devour all things, but your divine studies will flourish daily more and more and will free themselves from all danger of oblivion.

But I return to what I set out to say, that I thank you abundantly for being present today in such great numbers for my speech and for Bertucio, my kinsman, and for seeing fit to honor both of us with your illustrious presence. I promise that our unfailing loyalty and respect will never flag for you distinguished men as long as we both live. (1487)

I2

*Cassandra Fedele: Oration in Praise of Letters*
## Introduction

Even more clearly in this oration than in the preceding one, Cassandra identifies the study of the liberal arts with the improvement of character. She accepts
the classical definition of human beings as rational. It is our ability to learn which
distinguishes us from beasts. The more we learn the less like beasts we are, for
it makes us gentle, helpful to others, modest and pleasant. Using the example of
Philip of Macedon, she also identifies success in military prowess with learning.
Even though these two effects of learning might appear contradictory, Cassandra
was describing a combination that actually existed in numerous figures in Renaissance
Italy. One recalls also the military imagery applied to learned women, making
even stronger the analogy between learning and maleness.

In this latter connection the end of Cassandra's oration is poignant. She recognizes
that the study of letters offers no reward or dignity for a woman. She seems already,
in her early twenties, to have understood that there was no place for her to go
with her learning. Nonetheless, she loves it enough to say that, even so, a woman
should devote herself to learning. The pleasure and internal reward that come
from it are enough.

This translation is based on the Latin text in *Cassandra Fidelis Venetae epistolae
et orationes*, ed. Tomasini, pp. 201–7.

## Text

GIORGIO VALLA, THAT GREAT ORATOR and philosopher,[1] who found
me worthy of his attention, most serene Prince, Senators, and learned
men, encouraged and exhorted me—as I considered how women
could profit from assiduous study—thereby to seek immortality. Aware of the
weakness of my sex and the paucity of my talent, blushing, I decided to honor
and obey him inasmuch as he was demanding [something] honorable, in order
that the common crowd may be ashamed of itself and stop being offensive
to me, devoted as I am to the liberal arts. No one should be surprised, then,
if the mind and heart of her who now speaks hesitate a bit and falter. For
when I reflected upon the magnitude of the matter about which I had decided
to speak to this most distinguished and splendid assembly, I realized that nothing
could be so eloquent, distinguished and polished, even if presented by the most
eloquent speaker, that it would not seem threadbare, obscure, and mean in
comparison with the greatness of your knowledge and excellence. What woman,
I ask, has such force and ability of mind and speech that she could adequately
meet the standard of the greatness of letters or your learned ears? Thus daunted
by the difficulty [of the task] and conscious of my weakness, I might easily

have shirked this opportunity to speak, if your well-known kindness and clemency had not urged me to it. For I am not unaware that you are not in the habit of demanding or expecting from anyone more than the nature of the subject itself allows, or than a person's own strength can promise of them. Moreover, I am persuaded to speak on this matter by that which at first deterred me, your welcome courtesy and kindness, which encourages me to believe that no speech could be more pleasant and more agreeable to eloquent men (for you are all eloquent) and to those yearning for edification than one which in some way attests to and celebrates liberal arts and letters. Therefore, moved by these thoughts and by your attention to me, let me explain very briefly how useful and honorable the investigation of the LIBERAL ARTS is for man, and also how delightful and splendid.

Even an ignorant man – not only a philosopher – sees and admits that man is rightly distinguished from a beast above all by [his capacity of] reason. For what else so greatly delights, enriches and honors both of them than the teaching and understanding of letters and the liberal arts? Teaching and understanding indeed not only separate man decisively from beasts, but so clearly distinguish the man educated as befits a freeborn gentleman from ignorant and crude persons, that certainly, in my mind, portraits and shadows are no more distant from the living and real men they depict than are educated men from the unlearned and unskilled. Moreover, simple men, ignorant of literature, even if they have by nature this potential seed of genius and reason, leave it alone and uncultivated throughout their whole lives, stifle it with neglect and sloth, and render themselves unfit for greatness. For like wanderers they walk in darkness to all [life's] actions, and through imprudence, ignorance, and clumsiness, they are beset with calamities and, in a way, live a life of chance. These are they who make Fortune their goddess, place all their trust in her, and when she is favorable commend her [and] kiss her warmly, but when she is unfavorable, loudly accuse her and wail.

> Soldiers, who have conquered the worlds and on whom my destiny depends, behold the chance of battle you have so often prayed for. Prayer is no longer needed; with your swords you must now summon fate. So true to her bargains did fortune continue to the end the prosperity of Magnus; so true to her bargain she summoned him at his death from his pinnacle of glory and ruthlessly made him pay in a single day for all the disasters from which she protected him for so many years. And Pompey was the only man who never experienced good and evil together: his prosperity no god disturbed and on his misery no god had mercy. Fortune held her

hand for long and then overthrew him with one blow. He is tossed
on the sands.[2]

But learned men, filled with a rich knowledge of divine and human things,
turn all their thoughts and motions of the mind toward the goal of reason,
and thus free the mind, [otherwise] subject to so many anxieties, from all infir-
mity. No longer subject to the innumerable weapons of fortune, they are
fully prepared for living well and happily. They follow reason as a leader in
all things, considering not only their own welfare in any situation, but also
that of others, helping both privately and publicly, with diligent action and
[sound] advice. Hence Plato, a man almost divine, wrote that those republics
would be blessed either when those who administer them have been trained
in philosophy or when those trained in philosophy undertake their administra-
tion.[3] He observes, I believe, that men upon whom fortune has bestowed
physical well-being or wealth are much more prone to vice and more often
swayed by evil than those who have not been so privileged, and the goods
of the mind inborn by nature, if not cultivated through study, are wholly deficient; wherefore he did not consider the ignorant suited to conduct public
business.[4] And rightly so. The study of literature polishes intelligence, illuminates
and shapes the force of reason, either nearly erases or completely washes away
every blemish of soul, and richly perfects its endowments, and adds great ornament and beauty to the advantages of fortune and body. States and princes,
moreover, who favor and cultivate these studies become much more humane,
pleasing, and noble, and purely [by doing so] win for themselves a sweet reputation for humanity. Those whose minds are crude and rough naturally become
more civilized and polished by means of these studies, and often those who
are boastful, impudent, and wanton because of external goods [they have ob-
tained] or goods bestowed on them by nature, acquire from [the study of]
the liberal arts modesty, gentleness, and a certain wonderful kindness toward
all men. For just as places by nature rough and wild lie idle, but by the work
and care of men become not only fertile and fruitful but even delightful, likewise
our minds are refined, polished, and glorified by the good arts. Philip, King
of Macedon, understood this very well, by whose virtue and industry the
Macedonians had gained a rich empire and begun to rule over many peoples
and nations. In a letter to Aristotle the philosopher, in which he announced
that a son, Alexander, had been born to him, he said honorably and wisely
that he rejoiced far more that the child had been born at that period of Aristotle's life than that he had begotten the heir to so great an empire.[5] O excellent utterance and worthy of so great a ruler! O weighty imperial judgment!
For that king and emperor, exceptional for having spent the whole of his life
engaged in the business of war and victories, knew well that an empire could

hardly be rightly, prudently, and gloriously governed by one who had not been steeped in the best arts. Alexander proved this [principle] in his own case a little later. Instructed in liberal studies by Aristotle, he greatly excelled all princes and emperors either before or after him in ruling, maintaining, and increasing an empire. For this reason the ancients rightly judged all leaders deficient in letters, however skillful in military affairs, to be crude and ignorant. As for the utility of letters, enough said. Not only is this divine field, abundant and noble, amply useful, but it offers its copious, delightful, and perpetual fruits profusely. Of these fruits I myself have tasted a little and [have esteemed myself in that enterprise] more than abject and hopeless; and, armed with distaff and needle — woman's weapons — I march forth [to defend] the belief that even though the study of letters promises and offers no reward for women and no dignity, every woman ought to seek and embrace these studies for that pleasure and delight alone that [comes] from them.

# 13

## *Laura Cereta:*
## *Letter to Augustinus Aemilius,*
## *Curse against the Ornamentation of Women*

## *Introduction*

Laura Cereta wrote all the letters she published between July 1485 and March 1488, that is, when she was between the ages of sixteen and eighteen. The central event in her life during these years of letter-writing was her marriage to Pietro Serina, a local Brescian businessman, when she was fifteen. They had been married for only eighteen months when he died from the plague. Her letters are almost equally divided between those written before and those after his death. His death, and her reaction to it, provide one of the surest bases for dating her letters.

This particular letter was written about six months after her husband had died. She describes the scene at the beginning, but the grief is not so immediate as in some letters written nearer the time of his death. She recovered her spirits, as she says in another letter, not by weeping but by reason, that is, she immersed herself once again in writing, which she had temporarily abandoned after Pietro's death.

The three letters included in this anthology, though written as separate pieces, are all related and hence are grouped together. They reflect the values of a woman who has dedicated herself to learning and has to struggle against social pressures in doing so. Together they constitute one of the strongest assertions of women's intellects and the "right" of women to dedicate themselves to humanist studies to be found among learned women during the Quattrocento.

The body of this letter is taken up with a critique of the values of most of her peers who pay great attention to their looks (discussed here in great detail—with allusions to the satires of Juvenal). The last paragraph of the letter seems a complete turnabout, for Cereta apologizes for rather than berates her sex. The apology sounds very much like Isotta Nogarola's defense of Eve with which Cereta elsewhere shows herself familiar. The apology is, however, related to the beginning of the letter. The idea seems to be that just as Augustine should not praise her too highly, so he should not condemn others too harshly, for the same weak nature is operative in both. In this light, the critique which occupies the body of the letter must be read as a Christian complaint against pagan tendencies rather than as a brief in behalf of learning. This reflects the more religious posture Cereta admits she adopted for a time after her husband's death. In her subsequent letters, as we shall see, her attitude reflects much more her later return to learning as her major preoccupation.

The correspondent to whom this letter is written, Augustinus Aemilius, is unknown to us from other sources. Cereta wrote one other letter to him in addition to this one. The letter is written from the country, probably a country home belonging to her family. Why she was there we do not know. Perhaps it was to escape the innuendos of her critics, whom we shall meet in the following selection.

This translation is based on the Latin text published by J. F. Tomasini, *Laurae Ceretae epistolae* (Padua, 1640), pp. 66–70.

## Text

ALONE, I FLED TO THE COUNTRY, and in tranquil leisure delighted in [humane] studies. But you, meanwhile, were disturbed by my retreat, as if you seemed to consider me, a nonentity, important.[1]

I came at the end when my husband was feverish. Dying myself, I saw him half dead. I cheered him when he seemed to revive, I wept over him when he died, I fell lifeless on his dead body, and the fatal house which awaited me for marriage admitted me to lamentation. Thus one, and that an abominable year, saw me a girl, bride, widow, and pauper. These events were ordered by fate, not by you; you were mortal and died.

I thank you for esteeming me so highly, and more so than I deserve, for I cannot be compared to women like Sarah, Esther, Sephora and Susanna,[2] any more than a glowworm shining at night can be compared to the brilliant stars in heaven. I fear that your lofty opinion of me may spring from some other source than a carefully balanced judgment. Conjure up in your mind an ordinary woman, drab of face and drably dressed—for I care more for letters than for flashy clothes. Moreover, I have committed myself absolutely to that cultivation of virtue which can profit me not only when alive but also after death. There are those who are captivated by beauty. I myself should give the greater prize to grey-haired chastity, since in the lovely company of comely youth blaze up enticements to passion. For virtue excels the brilliance of beauty, elaborate polished artifice, and precious flowers of every tenderness. Let Mark Antony be attracted by bejewelled Cleopatra; I shall imitate the innocence of Rebecca.[3] Let Paris seek the wandering Helen; I choose to imitate the modesty of Rachel.[4] Wives are bewitched by rich display; more witless still are those who, to satisfy the appetite of their wives, destroy their patrimonies. Today men's love for women has made our commonwealth the imitator or rather the plunderer of the East. Luxury has thrived in this age, more than all others prodigiously vain. Let those who do not believe me attend the services of the church. Let them observe weddings packed with seated matrons.[5] Let them gaze at these women who, with majestic pride, promenade amidst crowds through the piazzas. Among them, here and there, is one who ties a towering knot—made of someone else's hair—at the very peak of her head;[6] another's forehead is submerged in waves of crimped curls; and another, in order to bare her neck, binds with a golden ribbon her golden hair. One suspends a necklace from her shoulder, another from her arm, another from neck to breast. Others choke themselves with pearl necklaces; born free, they boast to be held captive. And many display fingers glistening with jewels. One, lusting to walk more mincingly, loosens her girdle, while another tightens hers to make her breasts bulge. Some drag from their shoulders silken tunics. Others, sweet-scented with perfumes, cover themselves with an Arabian hood. Some boost themselves with high-heeled shoes. And all think it particularly modish to swathe their legs with fine soft cotton. Many press softened bread on their faces,[7] many artificially smooth their skin, stretched with wrinkles; there are few whose ruddy faces are not painted with the lustre of white lead. In one way or another they strive by means of exquisite artistry to seem more beautiful than the Author of their beauty decreed. The impudence of some women is shameful. They paint their white cheeks with purple and, with furtive winks and smiling mouths, pierce the poisoned hearts of those who gaze on them. O the bold wantonness of lost modesty! O the weakness of our sex, stooping to voluptuousness! We have only to hang from our ears little ornaments trembling with precious stones and emeralds, and we shall not differ from pagans. Was it for this, by chance, that we were begotten, that we might worship in shameless devotion the idols of our mirrored faces? Did we renounce display in baptism so that, as Christian women, we might imitate Jews and barbarians?

Even the feeblest desire [for honor] should make us blush over this longing for magnificence. These insane and lustful cravings, born of arrogance, should frighten us. Mindful of the ashes from which we come, we should renounce sins born from desires. How will our lamentations prevail if heavenly anger and indignation should rage against us miserable women? If those who rebel against the king commit their necks to the axe, why should we women marvel, rebels, indeed, warriors against God, if, to avenge our sin, an army rise up against us?[8] Rome mourns to this day the Gauls' assault. Italy, vanquished, bewails the Gothic sword. Greece suffers Mahomet's tyranny. These vicious devastations are not caused by human might but ordained by heaven [as a punishment for sins]. Let each woman dress and heal the wound from which we languish. We should seek the adornment of honor, not vulgar display,[9] and we should pursue this life mindful of our mortality. For God the Father has decreed that the good die well.

Therefore, Augustine, you have had ample opportunity to see that I consider this splendid magnificence foolish, and I wish you would pay no attention to my age or at least my sex. For [woman's] nature is not immune to sin; nature produced our mother [Eve], not from earth or rock, but from Adam's humanity. To be human is, however, to incline sometimes to good, but sometimes to pleasure. We are quite an imperfect animal, and our puny strength is not sufficient for mighty battles. [But] you great men, wielding such authority, commanding such success, who justly discern among your number so many present-day Brutuses, so many Curiuses, Fabriciuses, Catos, and Aemiliuses,[10] be careful: do not therefore be taken by the snare of this carefully arranged elegance. For where there is greater wisdom, there lies greater guilt.[11] February 12 [1487]

# 14

## Laura Cereta to Bibulus Sempronius:
## Defense of the Liberal Instruction of Women

## Introduction

As mentioned in the introduction to the preceding selection, Cereta recovered her spirits after her husband's death by immersing herself ever more deeply in her literary studies. These efforts, in turn, brought forth critics, both male and female, who, jealous of her accomplishments, belittled her work. Two principal charges were brought against her: that a woman could not be learned and that her father had written her letters for her. She turned against her critics with a ferocity at least equal to theirs. One of her surviving letters is an invective against two males whom she had known since childhood. But here we find, addressed to a man, as reasoned and thorough a defense of learned women as was penned during the Quattrocento. The letter is particularly interesting for its suggestion that the correspondent was disguising his contempt for women in singling out Cereta for praise.

The correspondent is unknown to us from other sources and may well be fictitious. "Bibulus," which we have not found elsewhere among the names of this period, means "drunkard." No other letter is addressed to such a correspondent.

This translation is based on the Latin text in Tomasini, *Laurae Ceretae epistolae*, pp. 187–95.

## Text

MY EARS ARE WEARIED BY YOUR CARPING. You brashly and publicly not merely wonder but indeed lament that I am said to possess as fine a mind as nature ever bestowed upon the most learned man. You seem to think that so learned a woman has scarcely before been seen in the world. You are wrong on both counts, Sempronius, and have clearly strayed from the path of truth and disseminate falsehood. I agree that you should be grieved; indeed, you should be ashamed, for you have ceased to be a living man, but have become an animated stone; having rejected the studies which make men wise, you rot in torpid leisure. Not nature but your own soul has betrayed you, deserting virtue for the easy path of sin.

You pretend to admire me as a female prodigy, but there lurks sugared deceit in your adulation. You wait perpetually in ambush to entrap my lovely sex, and overcome by your hatred seek to trample me underfoot and dash me to the earth. It is a crafty ploy, but only a low and vulgar mind would think to halt Medusa with honey.[1] You would better have crept up on a mole than on a wolf. For a mole with its dark vision can see nothing around it, while a wolf's eyes glow in the dark. For the wise person sees by [force of] mind, and anticipating what lies ahead, proceeds by the light of reason. For by foreknowledge the thinker scatters with knowing feet the evils which litter her path.

I would have been silent, believe me, if that savage old enmity of yours had attacked me alone. For the light of Phoebus cannot be befouled even in the mud.[2] But I cannot tolerate your having attacked my entire sex. For this reason my thirsty soul seeks revenge, my sleeping pen is aroused to literary struggle, raging anger stirs mental passions long chained by silence. With just cause I am moved to demonstrate how great a reputation for learning and virtue women have won by their inborn excellence, manifested in every age as knowledge, the [purveyor] of honor. Certain, indeed, and legitimate is our possession of this inheritance, come to us from a long eternity of ages past.

[To begin], we read how Sabba of Ethiopia, her heart imbued with divine power, solved the prophetic mysteries of the Egyptian Salomon.[3] And the earliest writers said that Amalthea, gifted in foretelling the future, sang her prophecies around the banks of Lake Avernus, not far from Baiae. A sibyl worthy of the pagan gods, she sold books of oracles to Priscus Tarquinius.[4] The Babylonian prophetess Eriphila, her divine mind penetrating the distant future, described the fall and burning of Troy, the fortunes of the Roman Empire, and the coming birth of Christ.[5] Nicostrata also, the mother of Evander, learned both in prophecy and letters, possessed such great genius that with sixteen symbols she first taught the Latins the art of writing.[6] The fame of Inachian Isis will also remain eternal who, an Argive goddess, taught her alphabet to the Egyptians.[7] Zenobia of Egypt was so nobly learned, not only in Egyptian, but also in Greek and Latin, that she wrote histories of strange and exotic places.[8] Manto of Thebes, daughter of Tiresias, although not learned, was skilled in the arts of divination from the remains of sacrificed animals or the behavior of fire and other such Chaldaean techniques. [Examining] the fire's flames, the bird's flight, the entrails and innards of animals, she spoke with spirits and foretold future events.[9] What was the source of the great wisdom of the Tritonian Athena by which she taught so many arts to the Athenians, if not the secret writings, admired by all, of the philosopher Apollo?[10] The Greek women Philiasia and Lasthenia, splendors of learning, excite me, who often tripped up, with tricky sophistries, Plato's clever disciples.[11] Sappho of Lesbos sang to her stone-hearted lover doleful verses, echoes, I believe, of Orpheus' lyre or Apollo's lute.[12] Later, Leontia's Greek and poetic tongue dared sharply to attack, with a lively and admired style, the eloquence of Theophrastus.[13] I should not omit Proba, remarkable for her excellent command of both Greek and Latin and who, imitating Homer and Virgil, retold the stories from the Old Testament.[14] The majesty of Rome exalted the Greek Semiamira, [invited] to lecture in the Senate on laws and kings.[15] Pregnant with virtue, Rome also gave birth to Sempronia, who imposingly delivered before an assembly a fluent poem and swayed the minds of her hearers with her convincing oratory.[16] Celebrated with equal and endless praise for her eloquence was Hortensia, daughter of Hortensius, an oratrix of such power that, weeping womanly and virtuous tears, she persuaded the Triumvirs not to retaliate against women.[17] Let me add Cornificia, sister of the poet Cornificius, to whose love of letters so many skills were added that she was said to have been nourished by waters from the Castalian spring; she wrote epigrams always sweet with Heliconian flowers.[18] I shall quickly pass by Tulliola, daughter of Cicero,[19] Terentia,[20] and Cornelia,[21] all Roman women who attained the heights of knowledge. I shall also omit Nicolosa [Sanuto] of Bologna, Isotta Nogarola and Cassandra Fedele of our own day.[22] All of history is full of these examples. Thus your nasty words are refuted by these arguments, which compel you to concede that nature imparts equally to all the same freedom to learn.

Only the question of the rarity of outstanding women remains to be addressed. The explanation is clear: women have been able by nature to be exceptional, but have chosen lesser goals. For some women are concerned with parting their hair correctly, adorning themselves with lovely dresses, or decorating their fingers with pearls and other gems. Others delight in mouthing carefully composed phrases, indulging in dancing, or managing spoiled puppies. Still others wish to gaze at lavish banquet tables, to rest in sleep, or, standing at mirrors, to smear their lovely faces. But those in whom a deeper integrity yearns for virtue, restrain from the start their youthful souls, reflect on higher things, harden the body with sobriety and trials, and curb their tongues, open their ears, compose their thoughts in wakeful hours, their minds in contemplation, to letters bonded to righteousness. For knowledge is not given as a gift, but [is gained] with diligence. The free mind, not shirking effort, always soars zealously toward the good, and the desire to know grows ever more wide and deep. It is because of no special holiness, therefore, that we [women] are rewarded by God the Giver with the gift of exceptional talent. Nature has generously lavished its gifts upon all people, opening to all the doors of choice through which reason sends envoys to the will, from which they learn and convey its desires. The will must choose to exercise the gift of reason.

[But] where we [women] should be forceful we are [too often] devious; where we should be confident we are insecure. [Even worse], we are content with our condition. But you, a foolish and angry dog, have gone to earth as though frightened by wolves. Victory does not come to those who take flight. Nor does he remain safe who makes peace with the enemy; rather, when pressed, he should arm himself all the more with weapons and courage. How nauseating to see strong men pursue a weakling at bay. Hold on! Does my name alone terrify you? As I am not a barbarian in intellect and do not fight like one, what fear drives you? You flee in vain, for traps craftily-laid rout you out of every hiding place. Do you think that by hiding, a deserter [from the field of battle], you can remain undiscovered? A penitent, do you seek the only path of salvation in flight? [If you do] you should be ashamed.

I have been praised too much; showing your contempt for women, you pretend that I alone am admirable because of the good fortune of my intellect. But I, compared to other women who have won splendid renown, am but a little mousling. You disguise your envy in dissimulation, but cloak yourself in apologetic words in vain. The lie buried, the truth, dear to God, always emerges. You stumble half-blind with envy on a wrongful path that leads you from your manhood, from your duty, from God. Who, do you think, will be surprised, Bibulus, if the stricken heart of an angry girl, whom your mindless scorn has painfully wounded, will after this more violently assault your bitter words? Do you suppose, O most contemptible man on earth, that I think myself sprung [like Athena] from the head of Jove? I am a school girl, possessed of the sleeping embers of an ordinary mind. Indeed I am too hurt, and my mind, offended, too swayed by passions, sighs, tormenting itself, conscious of the obligation to defend my sex. For absolutely everything—that which is within us and that which is without—is made weak by association with my sex.

I, therefore, who have always prized virtue, having put my private concerns aside, will polish and weary my pen against chatterboxes swelled with false glory. Trained in the arts, I shall block the paths of ambush. And I shall endeavor, by avenging arms, to sweep away the abusive infamies of noisemakers with which some disreputable and impudent men furiously, violently, and nastily rave against a woman and a republic worthy of reverence. January 13 [1488]

## 15

### Laura Cereta to Lucilia Vernacula: Against Women Who Disparage Learned Women

### Introduction

Not only did Cereta have to deal with carping men, she also had to contend with other women who attacked her out of envy and perhaps also because her accomplishment, so unusual for a woman, could easily be seen as socially deviant. Her departure from the norm of female existence invited resentment. This is perhaps why her tone is more violent here than in the preceding letter addressed to a man. Whereas in the preceding letter she appears to concentrate more on the issue at hand, here she focuses more on the persons involved. She regards learning as growing out of virtue, the external manifestation of an inward state. In effect she is saying that those who do not love learning have no inner direction of their own but are directed by things outside them. Thus, although virtue and learning are not the same thing, virtue will lead to learning rather than to the kinds of lives led by the women who criticize her.

This is the only letter addressed to this correspondent, who is unknown to us from other sources. Here again, the name may be fictitious. *Vernacula* can mean "common slave," perhaps "hussy."

This translation is based on the Latin text in Tomasini, *Laurae Ceretae epistolae*, pp. 122–25.

### Text

I THOUGHT THEIR TONGUES should have been fine-sliced and their hearts hacked to pieces—those men whose perverted minds and inconceivable hostility [fueled by] vulgar envy so flamed that they deny, stupidly ranting, that women are able to attain eloquence in Latin. [But] I might have forgiven those pathetic men, doomed to rascality, whose patent insanity I lash with unleashed tongue. But I cannot bear the babbling and chattering women, glowing with drunkenness and wine, whose impudent words harm not only our sex but even more themselves. Empty-headed, they put their heads together and draw lots from a stockpot to elect each other [number one];[1] but any women who excel they seek out and destroy with the venom of their envy. A wanton and bold plea indeed for ill-fortune and unkindness! Breathing viciousness, while she strives to besmirch her better, she befouls herself; for she who does not yearn to be sinless desires [in effect] license to sin. Thus these women, lazy with sloth and insouciance, abandon themselves to an unnatural vigilance; like scarecrows hung in gardens to ward off birds, they tackle all those who come into range with a poisonous tongue. Why should it behoove me to find this barking, snorting pack of provocateurs worthy of my forebearance, when important and distinguished gentlewomen always esteem and honor me? I shall not allow the base sallies of arrogance to pass, absolved by silence, lest my silence be taken for approval or lest women leading this shameful life attract to their licentiousness crowds of fellow-sinners. Nor should anyone fault me for impatience, since even dogs are permitted to claw at pesty flies, and an infected cow must always be isolated from the healthy flock, for the best is often injured by the worst. Who would believe that a [sturdy] tree could be destroyed by tiny ants? Let them fall silent, then, these insolent little women, to whom every norm of decency is foreign; inflamed with hatred, they would noisily chew up others, [except that] mute, they are themselves chewed up within. Their inactivity of mind maddens these raving women, or rather Megaeras,[2] who cannot bear even to hear the name of a learned woman. These are the mushy faces who, in their vehemence, now spit tedious nothings from their tight little mouths, now to the horror of those looking on spew from their lips thunderous trifles. One becomes disgusted with human failings and grows weary of these women who, [trapped in their own mental predicament], despair of attaining possession of human arts, when they could easily do so with the application of skill and virtue. For letters are not bestowed upon us, or assigned to us by chance. Virtue only is acquired by ourselves alone; nor can those women ascend to serious knowledge who, soiled by the filth of pleasures, languidly rot in sloth. For those women the path to true knowledge is plain who see that there is certain honor in exertion, labor, and wakefulness. Farewell. November 1 [1487]

# 16

## An Exchange of Letters between Cassandra Fedele and Alesandra Scala

## Introduction

Although these two letters are not responses to one another, they are related. The first letter shows the admiration in which Alessandra held Cassandra, which would have prompted her to ask the advice given in the second letter. Apart from a Greek epigram addressed to Angelo Poliziano, this letter is the only writing we know of from the pen of Alessandra.[1]

The question addressed in the second letter—whether marriage or studies is to be preferred by a learned woman—suggests that Alessandra had asked Cassandra to advise her. Cassandra's advice is interesting: choose that alternative to which nature more inclines you. The letter thus addresses directly the conflict learned women felt between learning and marriage—a conflict no learned man had to face.

This translation is based on the Latin text in Tomasini, *Cassandra Fidelis Venetae epistolae et orationes*, pp. 163–64 and p. 164 respectively.

## Text

### 16A: ALESSANDRA SCALA TO CASSANDRA FEDELE: CONGRATULATES HER ON HER GIFTS OF LEARNING AND PROMISES EQUAL DEDICATION

WHOEVER COMES TO [Florence] from [Venice] celebrates your virtue, so that now your name is revered here as much as there. Admirable and almost incredible things are told us about your intellect, learning, and manners. For this reason I congratulate you and give thanks, because you have made illustrious not only our sex but also this age. Florence, October 6, 1492

### 16B: CASSANDRA FEDELE TO ALESSANDRA SCALA: WHETHER MARRIAGE IS TO BE PREFERRED TO STUDIES BY A LEARNED WOMAN

FROM YOUR ELEGANT LETTER I saw and was pleased that you valued my good will, since you not only wished that I know all things about you but you also wished to consult me about a personal concern. And so, my Alessandra, you are of two minds, whether you should give yourself to the Muses or to a man. In this matter I think you must choose that to which nature more inclines you. For Plato states that all advice which is received, is received in proportion to the readiness of the receiver.[2] You

must certainly be prepared to make a sound judgment and not act impetuous-
ly. February 15, 1492

# Part III

# Men to Women

## 17

*Gregorio Correr: Letter to the virgin Cecilia,
on Fleeing this worldly Life*

## Introduction

The author of this letter, Gregorio Correr (1409–64) was a Venetian patrician, humanist, and theologian. He studied under Vittorino (1425–29), under whose tutelage he wrote the famous tragedy *Progne*, mentioned in his letter to Cecilia. In 1431 he entered holy orders, was named apostolic notary by his relative Pope Eugenius IV before March 1433, and was made in later years commendatory abbot of San Zeno in Verona (1443) and patriarch of Venice (1464) shortly before his death that same year. In 1433 he attended the Council of Basel, where he discovered Salvianus' *De divina providentia*, also mentioned in this letter.[1] The letter was written in 1443.

Cecilia, as mentioned in her biography, also studied with Vittorino. His relationship to the Gonzaga children has been captured in a letter written by the Florentine monk and humanist, Ambrogio Traversari, who once visited the school.

> Vittorino is staying at Goito in charge of the Gonzaga children. . . . The children seem to be on the happiest terms with him. We talked together for several hours. Then one of the boys declaims some two hundred lines which he had composed upon the state entry of the Emperor Sigismund into Mantua. I was astonished by the taste and scholarship displayed not less than by the grace and propriety of delivery. Two younger brothers [Gianlucido and Alessandro] and their sister [Cecilia] were of the party, all bright and intelligent children. . . .[2]

In another passage Traversari attests that Cecilia (as well as her brothers) wrote in Greek as well as in Latin.[3] Cecilia's accomplishments, which were notable and unusual, were not directly known to Gregorio for, as he says in this letter, when he was a student under Vittorino, Cecilia had just come into the world. And later he says that he has heard she is an accomplished poet. He knows, nonetheless, the ambience in which she lives, both in the school and in the court. These are alluded to at various points in the letter.

This letter is directly related to Cecilia's intention to enter a convent. When her wish was strongly opposed by her father (at one point even by violence), Vittorino entered the lists in favor of Cecilia's expressed intention. In the spring of 1443 he escorted Lady Paola, Cecilia's mother, to Rome, probably in connection with Cecilia's intention, which her mother favored. On the way to Rome, Vittorino and Lady Paola stopped in Florence. It was here that Correr held a conference with Paola on the subject of Cecilia's desire. At the urging of Vittorino — as Correr states at the beginning of this letter — he wrote to Cecilia in an effort to add another persuasive opinion in favor of her intention.

Cecilia entered a convent in 1444, after her father's death. Her mother Paola entered with her (Paola had founded the convent). Given the devoutly religious nature of both mother and daughter, there is little doubt that her motives were genuinely religious. But the question still arises of whether she entered the convent solely for religious reasons or because it provided her solace and the only acceptable context for her studies. Woodward comments in this connection: "We must remember that apart from its attraction for a devout spirit the religious life was still the one sure refuge to a woman of studious instincts."[4] In the letter here translated there is also an interesting passage which leaves many questions unanswered. Correr says that Cecilia's father had agreed that she no longer had to marry but nonetheless asked that she remain at court and not enter a religious life. If this were the case, it would appear to have been the kind of arrangement Cecilia would have liked had she wanted to pursue a life of scholarship. For presumably she would now be free. Correr may have misperceived the situation, for he was, after all, not an "insider" in the household. But his response is nonetheless significant. He cannot at all understand the father's position, for it would make his daughter vulnerable to the world. The point, of course, is that while such an attitude presented no great barrier for males, it presented an insuperable one for females, for women could live socially acceptable lives in marriage or in a convent, but not outside either.

At the same time, it is significant that Correr does not discuss solely the religious life and its advantages — though he dwells at length on the superiority of virginity over marriage and on the trials and temptations of life in the world, which are characteristic of treatises on the contempt of the world. He also discusses Cecilia's curriculum of study in the convent, suggesting that he understood study as one of her principal aims. Correr had himself entered the religious life in part to escape the claims of state service placed on a Venetian aristocrat. Perhaps he saw in Cecilia's desire an intention similar to his own. One can only believe that there was a kinship of spirit between them in this respect.

Nonetheless, when the plan of study itself is scrutinized, Boccaccio's notion that poetry is disguised theology (making possible an almost complete appropriation of the pagan tradition by Christians) is not visible. Correr advises Cecilia to put away her Virgil and her Cicero and to take up, instead, Christian authors. Throughout the letter, as a perusal of the notes will make clear, he cites Scripture and Christian authors, and only on three or four occasions quotes Virgil or alludes to other pagan authors. Indeed, he even suggests that Cecilia might find a way to "translate" Virgil into Christian terms with some judicious changes in his wording.

Although both Correr and Gonzaga entered the religious life, there was a great difference in their life-styles, as reflected both in their respective careers and in Correr's advice in this letter. Correr, in his religious vocation, was still able to function in the world, to move about among ecclesiastics and humanists. None of that was possible for Gonzaga. For her, as for women in general, the sacrifice had to be much greater.

This translation is based on the Latin text in G. B. Contarini, *Anecdota Veneta* (Venice, 1757), pp. 33–44.[5]

## *Text*

WHEN RECENTLY I VISITED that glorious woman, your mother, in Florence, after some small talk we came to the subject of your holy decision, namely, that having repudiated an earthly marriage, you have chosen a heavenly spouse and, scorning and abjuring this world, you long for the convent with all the strength of your heart. The only thing which stands in your way is the opposition of your father—and I do not say "your parents," since she, the mirror of all holiness, would rather behold you as the bride of Christ than see the progeny of your body. Holding this attitude, she loves you the more, exceeding her husband in strength of soul, which is usually weaker in the female sex. I thanked our God, from whom comes every finest favor and every perfect gift. I praised your decision and I counseled hope—since this is not a matter pertaining to the salvation of your soul alone, but also to those of many virgins who will be drawn by your glorious and rare example to the fruit of a better life. "Why don't you therefore write something to our Cecilia?" asked our teacher Vittorino. For he was standing beside me weeping with joy, as usual, "for your style is effective for this type of exhortation." I believe the pious father inferred this from a certain letter I wrote about ten years ago now to a Carthusian novice and sent to him to read.[6] But O my foolish exhortations! O vain hopes! O futile human efforts! He returned to the world. "Unless the Lord build the house, they labor in vain who build it."[7] But such complaints should not cloud my opening words. Rather, I shall attempt in this discourse, of which you are the spur, to encourage you in your decision, insofar as God grants it. And indeed, warned by Vittorino, I have not written this in haughty pride, but ask that you read this letter in the same spirit of charity in which it is written and that you not measure by the deficiency of my skill the extent of that charity.

Many excellent teachers of the Christian religion, who were by merit of their sanctity and learning the glorious lights of the church, have, in letters sent to holy virgins, advised them of their mission, of their studies, of their virtues. Among these are those celebrated letters of Jerome to the virgins Eustochia and Demetrias and, likewise, of Ambrose to Demetrias.[8] Many also have in various treatises discussed holy virginity and continence, and the excellence of both, as did Augustine,[9] and Basil in that work which Fra Ambrogio recently translated into Latin, whom for his good merits may God reward in heaven. Indeed, he has translated superbly many useful things from the teachers of the church, and he would have translated more if premature death had not released him from human labors.[10] Why need I mention the others? Their writings in part still survive, in part have perished through our negligence, as may be seen by consulting the catalogues of ecclesiastical writers. No other works will you find equally celebrated [in the history of] thought and letters. Once holy and eloquent men delighted to exhort virgins, to instruct them in wisdom, to laud holy virginity. It was also necessary to defend the merits of virginity against the savage barkings of the heretics. For there were certain monsters of men who spread impious and false opinions concerning the Holy Trinity and other mysteries of God and the Church. Some indeed were so shameless (among these the chief was Jovinian) that they dared to prefer marriage to virginity. Their impiety the Catholic teachers refuted in several books.[11] Whatever then can be thought or said concerning virginity, whatever can be adduced from the testimony of sacred writings, is contained in their letters. Thus studious virgins should be directed to the wellsprings of these writers and should pass over the little trickling streams [of knowledge possessed by lesser authors]. For what can I add, or those like me—sinners, that is to say, and inexpert in divine scriptures—amid this abundance, this authority, this effulgence of excellent writings?

O excellent gift of God! O virginity akin to the angels and consecrated in the Virgin Mother and in the Virgin's Son! You are the road to heaven, the enemy of demons, the ornament of the soul, the splendor and the crown of modesty, you rest in the bosom of God, you follow the Lamb, as it says in the Apocalypse of St. John: "These are they who were not defiled with women; for they are virgins. These follow the Lamb wherever he goes."[12] By these words, Virgin Cecilia of Christ, do not suppose that women are neglected but that both sexes are understood where the male sex alone is mentioned. Concerning this matter the Lord spoke in the gospel: "Not all can accept this teaching; but those to whom it has been given."[13] And a little later he adds: "Let him accept it who can."[14] And [there is a fuller explanation] in Corinthians: "Now concerning virgins I have no commandment of the Lord, yet I give an opinion." "I wish all men to be as I am."[15] And in the following passage: "And the unmarried woman, and the virgin, thinks about the things of the Lord, that she may be holy in body and spirit. Whereas she who is married thinks

about the things of the world, how she may please her husband."[16] You see
how far virginity exceeds matrimony, as far, evidently, as it is better to think
of those things which are of the Lord, that you may sanctify body and spirit,
than of those things which are of the world, that you may please a husband.
Quite rightly, then, is inviolate virginity preferred to marriage. So may they
with profound humility yearn for such a good to whom it has been granted
to attain God's great mercy by such excellent service as this. And of marriage,
permitted because of the frailty of the human condition for the propagation
of the species, holy virginity is the most beautiful and finest fruit. Say, therefore,
with the [Psalmist]: "Gladly will I offer sacrifice to thee."[17] The merit of this
is the more sublime because the sacrifice is voluntary, inasmuch as she has
the power to choose the path of marriage, in accordance with the indulgence.
He says: "And if a virgin marries, she has not sinned. Yet such will have tribulation of the flesh."[18] Does it interest you to know what kind of tribulation?
Hear the Lord's curse on Eve: "I will greatly multiply your pain in childbearing; in pain you shall bring forth children, and you shall be under your husband's power, and he shall rule over you."[19] From this condemnation virgins
are free, subject not to men but to God alone. But since I do not want to
appear to accuse nature, I shall pursue no further the defects of marriage and
related matters—which should not be discussed with a virgin—of the sort of
which your countryman Virgil wrote: "This is the tenth month now, and she
is sick of waiting."[20]

Of what, then, shall I speak? Shall I praise your lofty nature? Shall I wonder
that a noble virgin, brought up in the fortunate house of her princely father
among exquisite delights, of uncommon beauty of body, in the flower of her
age, should suddenly abjure the world's pomp and a pending marriage? Have
the will of her father, of her brothers, the prayers of her youthful spouse, counted
for nothing? Has nothing moved this virgin's soul, not the tears of her nurse
which flow for you, I know, as though you were already dead—such is the
foolish affection of this sort of woman? You have spurned all things for the
love of Christ. Amid your father's great wealth you are poor. At sumptuous
feasts you fast. Within magnificent walls you dream of the convent. You see
your ladies dressed in precious robes and the purple which you have rejected,
and they, like wanton women, mock your humble habit with surreptitious
jeers. These things, you are aware, are godly and worthy of praise, fine matter
for rhetoricians. But they should not be addressed to you by an ecclesiastical
man, if indeed I deserve to be called a man of the church, for I did not intend
to write you a panegyric. If perhaps I later write something about you to others,
I shall do so to inspire other virgins and to rebuke, by setting you up as an
example, the luxury and wantonness of many women.

But since I am not going to write at greater length about the duties of virgins or virginity itself, nor to you about yourself, that is, in praise of you, it remains for me to list your difficulties and perils and to demonstrate that you are not yet firmly settled so long as you remain in your father's house, far from the convent—as though, when you had started a journey through rugged mountains, I were trying to lead you down to the smooth plains, where there is less danger of falling. Indeed, I should better have written these things to your father so that he might finally be persuaded to give in to your prayers—I should say, to stop defying the Holy Spirit. For I hear that you are burning with great love for this very thing to happen. I marvel, however, since he is a wise man, that once he had permitted you to rescind the marriage agreement and to commit yourself to virginity, he could not see that the palace of a secular prince, however modest, was an alien home for your ambition. But he is your father, he wants to see his daughter, he wants to speak to her. But who would sail in winter past rocky cliffs amid pirates when he could enjoy a safe lodging—and then, though it were unnecessary, take his daughter with him? Would he not prefer her to be safe, though distant, than to see her in danger? Unless perhaps he deems the perils of the soul less terrible than those of the body. If he loves her, why does he delay his daughter's departure? Does he think that he should be loved more than God by his daughter, or his daughter by him? The Lord declares in the gospel: "He who loves father or mother more than me is not worthy of me; and he who loves son or daughter more than me is not worthy of me."[21] But he must not think that his daughter is more loved by him than by God. The fact that he was opposing your suggestion by holding up the pretext of marriage did have some semblance of reasonableness. He was hoping for grandchildren, the augmentation of his house, a bond with an illustrious family; and yet all of these ought to be repudiated for the sake of the good coming from virginity. But when he had conceded that you need not marry, why he continued to deny what was the consequence of that decision—that having renounced the marriage you would then in turn renounce the world—this I do not understand. If virgins destined to have mortal spouses are by their parents' scrupulous care shut off from the sight of men, how much more should they be secluded from the sight of the world if they are to celebrate an immortal marriage with a heavenly spouse? What will you, a virgin devoted to God, do in the world? If you are a bride of Christ, "forget thy people and thy father's house."[22] Follow him where he can be found more easily. He who was born in a manger rarely enters haughty palaces. Christ, a pauper, must be sought in a humble dwelling. "Those clothed in delicate garments are in the palaces of kings."[23] You have stripped off your delicate garments; now leave the house of the prince. In any case, I do not summon you to the desert, nor invite you to dine on the locusts of John and to clothe yourself in camel's hair,[24] but to the convent, where you may escape the spectacle of the world.

Do you think you can stay in your father's house and not be moved by the many storms of secular life? How can a man hide fire in his own breast or walk on live coals and not be burned? And how can he touch pitch and not be soiled? Ah! "The life of man upon earth is a warfare."[25] Do you think that we [pledged to a holy life] do not have to struggle against the stubborn and unruly flesh? Hear the apostle: "I see," he says, "another law in my members warring against the law of my mind and making me prisoner of the law of sin."[26] Thus the vessel of election [Paul] controlled his body with toil, with hardship, with vigils, with hunger and thirst, with many fasts, with cold and nakedness, lest he be a hypocrite when he preached to others.[27] "I know this," you say, "I, too, shall fast." They will not permit it. Believe me, Cecilia, in fasting the visage pales, the skin wrinkles, the body shrivels to gauntness, weakened limbs take faltering steps. They will not wait for these signs in you, but if, for some reason, you seem a little pale, without delay a senate of doctors will be consulted, your ladies will run hither and thither, your nurse will coddle you, a soft bed will be made for you, and you will be laid upon it, the doctors will feel your arteries, dreaming up meanwhile some way to flatter your watching parents. Having consulted among themselves, they turn to your father. "This maiden of yours," they say, "fasts too much, keeps too many vigils, against the rules of Hippocrates, wherefore her stomach has become irritated and she has fallen into a fever." Meanwhile, you will be hounded with a storehouse of delicacies, until they prescribe something to drink. Are we to believe in Chiron, then, or Melampus, and not in that Samaritan who placed on his ass the man beaten by robbers, poured oil and wine on his wounds, persuades us to bear the cross, to vigils, and to prayer, lest we enter into temptation?[28] [Are we not to believe] in the apostle who says "mortify your members,"[29] and "it is good not to eat meat and not to drink wine."[30] For what purpose, Jerome, did you go forth into that vast solitude to be burned by the heat of the sun? Why did you neglect your skin until your flesh was as black as an Ethiopian's? Why did you bruise your shattered body on the bare earth? Why did you bathe in cold water and tremble to taste cooked meat? The mind, he replies, rages with desire even when the body is frozen, and in a man whose flesh is dead before its time there still boil up vital fires of lust.[31] What torments of temptation, then, will we suffer amid comforts, if holy men leading lives of extreme austerity suffer these?

You will be summoned, moreover, to the parties of your brothers, your father commanding you to attend, so that it would be undutiful to refuse. His daughters-in-law will be summoned too, and you will come, will sit among them. The dangerous dinner will be served. Handsome youths will tend you, tasting each dish first for your safety. You will see yourself in a mirror of golden vessels, will gaze upon walls patterned with intricate designs, will hear the flutists play. Several wines will be produced, exquisite foods, to which the gullet has given diverse names. And servant girls will come to mix you rich wine, for you will not even be allowed to mix your own. What will you do amid this luxury? I know: you will lower your eyes, you will tremble to touch these poisons of the soul, remembering how young Daniel shunned those royal repasts and Elijah ascended the mountain, not [indulging in] rich banqueting but [subsisting on] water and ash-baked bread.[32] "So you condemn the banquets of your relatives?" perhaps will be the remark made by one of those men of the church who will shamelessly pay gold for an especially fine fish or who compete with laymen in the luxury of their banquets—whose celebrations, you would think if you were to enter their homes, are bacchanals—while Christ, thirsty, in the person of his poor, languishes outside the proud and shuttered gates. I shall respond: "I shall always condemn your banquets. More modest ones I do not condemn, but I fear them." Read what was written about the saintly Job: "And his sons went and made a feast by houses everyone in his day. And sending they called their three sisters to eat and drink with them. And when the days of their feasting were gone about, Job sent to them, and sanctified them, and rising up early offered burnt offerings for everyone of them. For he said: 'Lest perhaps my sons have sinned.'"[33] Thus the prudent father feared the sins that might occur in banqueting, just as elsewhere it is written: "It is better to go to the house of mourning than to go to the house of feasting."[34] Nor were appetites in those times tempted by so many delicacies, nor the cooks skilled in so many arts. Marcus Apicius, his patrimony consumed, had not yet published that infamous book on the seasoning of foods.[35]

In saying these things, I do not imply that your behavior lacks modesty. I know your parents, I know your brothers, I know your domestic routine and the discipline of your family, having studied for two years in my early adolescence in your house under the preceptor Vittorino, at the time when you were born. But in princes' houses, magnificent objects are seen which bespeak not luxury, but splendor and liberality. I know that there is in that house no lascivious dress or song or indecency in speech. Among the young servant boys and girls, there is no impudence or wantonness, but only modesty and honesty. Jesters, parasites, seductive lutenists, and such unworthy members of humankind have no place in your home, such people as, I am ashamed to say, are considered to be delights in most princely houses, and domestic vices are considered to be inescapably human. But since even in well-regulated princely homes it is not considered improper to dance in elaborate rings to the music of flutes and to sing frivolous songs, you will hear of these

things also in your father's house, even if you don't see them. Far be it from
me to suppose that a virgin devoted to God in so modest a home is invited
to view such things — which appeal to many shameless members of my own
class as well. I speak of churchmen. Flee, Cecilia, virgin of Christ, flee, cover
your eyes, cover your ears. Flee, if you can, to where neither song nor sym-
phony are heard. But you will find it hard to escape them in your father's
palace. There, moreover, you will hear the gossip of old women in whose
loquacity there is sin. You will have to keep company with new brides, you
will see your brothers' wives decked out with coronets, gold, gems, and robes
embellished with a veil of gold.[36] You will see their swelling bellies, and more,
you will visit them when they are in labor. For I do not suggest that you shun
human responsibilities. And one of your ladies will bring you a red and naked
newborn infant and will say "behold, you have a little nephew," and will give
it to you to be nurtured in your bosom. These things, believe me, disturb
a virgin's studies, disturb her mind. The heart of man is unstable and is easily
seduced from hardship to ease. "For the flesh lusts against the spirit."[37] "Because
all that is in the world is the lust of the flesh, and the lust of the eyes, and
the pride of life."[38] What today has not moved you will sway you tomorrow.
Mountains are toppled, stars fall from heaven, [and] water, the softest of things,
over the space of long years will penetrate stone. And will not a flood of temptations move a virgin's heart? Do you think the devil, who is accustomed to
tear down mountains and to drag stars down from the sky — that is, to entice
holy men to a sinful fall — who, not by those songs of which the poet spoke,
"his music was able even to draw down the moon from heaven,"[39] but by secret
temptings, persuades people to commit rape and adultery — do you think the
devil has no hope of luring one girl, as long as you are in the world, to marriage? Alas! What triumphal processions would the victor lead through hell
if he could snare a bride of Christ and wed her to a mortal husband — which
may God forbid. For even if you have not dedicated yourself to virginity by
entering a convent, yet you must know that your holy spouse, who sees into
the secret places of the heart, holds as valid the intention of your mind. For
what would be the source of your great strength to stand firm against the will
of your father if you had not made a solemn mental pledge of virginity? This
strength your heavenly father multiplied in opposition to the father of your
flesh, whose soul he inclined to your just wishes, so that you might implore
him with unceasing prayers for that which you still desire. For it is written:
"As the divisions of waters, so the heart of the king is in the hand of the Lord."[40]
You have put your hand to the plough and must not look back. Remember
Lot's wife who, as long as she followed her husband, avoided all dangers, but
when forgetful and vanquished in her soul, could not keep her eyes from burning Sodom, and as a consequence left a powerful example to posterity.[41] You

have fled from the midst of the wedding as though from a fire on the mountain of virginity to avoid looking back upon the world. How many holy virgins,
do you believe, have been inspired by your example? How many convents
petition the Lord with assiduous prayers for you to join them? They will call
blessed those whom the Lord deems worthy of your company. But what if
they should hear of a marriage? First, they would not believe it. Later, overcome by tears, with what lamentations would they grieve your loss! And men
of the world would say that, earlier, it was not marriage which you had rejected but your betrothed.

Ah, therefore, little novice in Christ, ask your Lord God with your whole
heart that he may sway your father's mind, He who once, in response to the
prayer of the virgin Cecilia, his martyr, whose name and virginity you bear,
summoned from marriage to the grace of baptism and to martyrdom a
bridegroom burning in his lust for her flesh.[42] Implore the aid of the most
merciful Mother of God, the eternal Virgin Mary, who grants the prayers
of none more joyfully than of those who wish to guard fragile virginity. And
kneeling before your father, speak bravely: "I ask you, father, in the name
of your concern, if you have any, for my salvation, for the hope of the blessed
life, for the charity by which God loved us, sending his Son for the redemption of our souls, do not let your daughter remain in peril for so long among
the sirens of the world. For why do I perceive with these eyes, by which I
yearn to see Christ, so many enticements of the secular life? If, after you have
been raised up from human concerns, I am to seek the convent, why may
I not rather seek it now, while you are alive and willing? If you had pledged
me to a mortal husband far across the seas, then you would certainly have
sent me to a remote land and would never see your daughter again. Now because
I hasten to a heavenly spouse, it displeases you to be separated from me by
mere walls and partitions. If we should so decide, [dwelling] in the same city,
we would be enclosed by the same walls. You have the consolations of this
life: wife, sons, daughters-in-law, grandsons. My other sister you gave to the
world, and she has left you [for she has died] a sweet little grandson. Why,
among so many dear loved ones, am I alone desired? Why am I held back
against my will? Why is a tiny cell begrudged me, and the meagre table of
the humble family of Christ? Let me go where the prayers of your daughter
may more easily reach the ears of the divine majesty, to make constant in-
tercessions on your behalf. If you will permit me to go, the dowry agreed
upon for an earthly marriage I shall hand over to Christ, lay it up for treasures
in heaven, bequeath to the poor."

By these arguments and others like them, I hope your father (for he is not
made of iron) can be moved. Add to your pleas those of your ally, your mother,
and those of Vittorino, and show him this letter of mine, if you think it says

anything worthwhile. But if he cannot be swayed, would I stay or would I go away without the knowledge of my father? – since in Mantua, without his permission, I could not be admitted to a monastery. I know that for the sake of God one must fly in one way or another to the banner of Christ, leaving parents, homeland, and all things. Did I say without your father's knowledge? Nay, even trampling on him, or deceiving him, if it be necessary. But what I might unhesitatingly urge upon one of more robust age and masculine sex I do not dare urge upon a young virgin. I spare your age, I spare your modesty, I spare your sex. I prefer that you stay in your father's house, lest any sinister rumor about a bride of Christ arise, and lest your example teach girls, on the pretext of religion, to dream of flight. Remain, rather, in your father's house but, as much as it is possible to do so, as though in a convent. Venerate your mother as though an abbess. If from maternal love she presses some luxury upon you, decline with an explanation humbly offered. From her table feed your slight body as much as is necessary to health; that much also allow to sleep. With your mother attend divine services; never visit churches or convents without her. Do not yourself choose a priest to confess to, but let your mother choose him. And let her also choose your companions. I am spared the burden of giving much advice by the well-tested common sense of that most pious woman. Pray frequently; with diligent reading feed your soul.

Be certain not to embroider anything for secular use. And I recommend that you weave with coarse rather than fine cloth [and] that before long you procure a holy comb, so that you may always be busy. For I don't want you to be like Lyda or the many virgins of the world who think that their finger tips deserve to touch nothing but silk and purple and gold cloth.[43] Just because you possess nobility or virginity or knowledge of letters – which is, in a girl, considered a miracle in our age – be sure not to scorn anyone lacking in these gifts. Consider her more noble who makes greater progress in the spiritual life, who, while pleasing to the eyes of God, appears to herself contemptible. Compete with such women in humility. Let the less perfect women learn humility from you. Admit no one to your company who uses powder or a mirror; let their character be enough makeup for them. Let none praise your intelligence in your presence, and much less the loveliness of your body. Let none call you "illustrious," none "lady," and none revere you with bent knee. Let there be no word among you of marriage. Leave such knowledge to others who marry, who swell in pregnancy, to whom infants wail from the cradle, of whom the apostle writes: "Being idle, they learn to go about from house to house, and are not only idle but gossipers as well and busybodies, mentioning things they ought not."[44] Let your conversation be serious and modest. Speak of the mercies of God, of the glory of the saints, of sacred virgins, of the constancy of martyrs, of faith, hope and charity, and of the other virtues. Beyond this, the splendid works of the saints will teach you what you should do and not do, especially those of Jerome, of which I am sending you a selection. Let the precepts which I have written be enough for you to follow while you are in your father's house. When you have entered the convent, however, which you ought to choose with your mother's guidance—for you will do so, I suspect, by the grace of God, not too long from now—I leave you to be instructed in sacred learning by experienced virgins. And do not expect me, in the meantime, to describe for you the form of the religious life, which you will learn from these women and which you will be able to read for yourself and understand better and better as you make progress. But how much more successfully one may pursue this life in a well-run convent than in the world you can judge by considering what was said earlier.

Moreover, many have written of the benefits of the regulated life, and I also in the abovementioned letter to the Carthusian novice. Oh, if I could carry you across our lagoons as though you were escaping from Egypt across the Red Sea, to the Convent of Sant'Andrea in Venice which, now in its ninetieth year under the rule of St. Augustine, is considered the most religious of all, I would not fear the pursuing Pharaoh, doomed with his army to drown. Good Jesus! What young vines spring forth there from the Lord's vineyard, which the fertile soil fructifies in paradise! What ranks of angels there! What consolation of the Holy Spirit! What exaltations of souls to God, and how many! What tears, what joy!

Here I can consecrate in words the memory of my gentle Beriola, so that you may learn about the sanctity of many from the sanctity of one. She, born of our family, was among the first of those venerable handmaidens of Christ who, in that same place where now the convent is, before they undertook the religious life, combined their patrimonies to run a hospice for poor women, giving witness in good works, according to the apostle's edict.[45] Like mothers, like sisters, they cared for these women. Moreover, they sought alms from virtuous households. When Beriola was returning from a mission of this kind, she set out and stopped at a small inn to arrange for transportation across the lagoon, as she was accustomed to do. She saw no oarsman in the boat, and there was need of haste. She drew her cloak from her shoulders, therefore, and, unfurling it like a sail, embarked confidently upon the waters following the sign of the cross and so reached the other bank by the oar of faith. But no wonder! "The right hand of the Lord has done mightily."[46] This faithful woman did not doubt, for she knew that Peter began to sink when he doubted, and the Lord, walking upon the waters, rebuked him.[47]

There remains [something to be said about your studies]. I forbid utterly the reading of secular literature, particularly the works of the poets. For how

can I believe that you have renounced the world if you love the things which
are of the world? What does it matter what form your love for the world
takes? Certainly you love the world if you love worldly literature. Laymen
can be forgiven if, having at least given up indecent writers, they continue
to study others. [But] a bride of Christ may read only sacred books and ecclesiastical writers. So you must put aside your beloved Virgil, with Vittorino's
pardon. Take up instead the Psalter [and], instead of Cicero, the Gospel. Believe
me, I speak from experience: even if secular literature causes no harm beyond
this, it leads the mind away from divine reading. You have in ecclesiastical
writers, if you require it, the highest eloquence. Turn to the books of Lactantius, Cyprian, Hilary, Jerome, Ambrose, Augustine, Gregory, Leo, Cassian,
Sulpitius, Bernard, and Salvianus also, whose books *On the Providence of God*
I brought back with me from German dungeons to Italy on my return from
the Council of Basel.[48] Is there not found here such eloquence that there is
no need to seek from the heathen words which delight and persuade? Read
these, therefore, and those works which have been translated from the Greek
teachers, by Gregory, Basil, Chrysostom, Athanasius, and John called Climacus,
and also Ephraem Syrus.[49] Many others could be named if it were my purpose to assemble for you a catalogue of ecclesiastical writers. Why, therefore,
do we seek out an alien eloquence when we enjoy such an abundance of our
own Christian eloquence? You should also consider alien those nursery tales
and dreamers' fantasies, such as that book by I don't know which silly woman
entitled *A Mirror of Simple Souls.*[50] Repudiate such books. You should read
nothing that is not used and approved by the learned. You have the writings
of the saints in which you may delight, on which you may nourish your soul.
Read these. Moreover, do not scorn to excerpt their best passages and translate
them into the vernacular for the edification of unlettered virgins. But to go
back to my recommendations for the best works to read, I suggest that you
learn intimately the books of Augustine. So melodious, surely, is that man's
style, so full of grace his exposition of Scripture, so intelligent his discussion
of divine matters, so broad his erudition, so forceful his mind, that in wondrous ways you may profit from reading him. Now his discourse will so lift
your soul up to celestial heights that it will forget its mortal burden and will
be wholly rapt in God. Now he will dissolve your heart in sweet fountains
of tears, now he will draw forth bitter tears of repentance, now he will move
you to hope for heaven, now he will make you fear Gehenna, now he will
delight, now he will edify with his vast learning. He wrote so many works
for the edification of the children of the church, disputed so many issues against
the heretics, expounded so many passages from the canonical books, that the
studious reader would scarcely be able to finish reading all his books.

Moreover, since I have heard that you write poetry not inelegantly, this pursuit also I advise you to put to the use of religion and piety. It may be pleasant for you, having spurned worldly verse, to sing Hosanna with the children of the Hebrews: now to celebrate in verse Mary's manger, the fields of Bethlehem, graced with the Lord's cradle; now the flowing Jordan and the waters upon which the Lord walked with dry feet; now the Mount of Olives and the hill of Calvary and the victory of the Cross; now the Lord himself storming the gates of hell, the bolts of the inferno, rising from the dead, ascending to heaven; now depicting the victories of the martyrs, now the virgins' crowns. You have the example of Christian poets who have sung of ecclesiastical things and the Gospels themselves. Damasus [the Roman pope], according to Jerome, delighted in the study of poetry, as did many of the Greeks.[51] Our Ambrose wrote lovely hymns, and Hilary, too, did not disdain poetry, as witnessed by the verses he addressed to his daughter.[52]

Though I do not suggest that you take the opportunity to read the secular poets, and to wish to imitate the intellectual Proba, yet if any of their writings you once learned should happen to come to mind (since we do not easily forget those things with which we were imbued at a tender age), I do not forbid you to apply to the Church any verse which spontaneously suggests itself, as certain of our Christian poets did most elegantly. "Christ, help ever-present in man's dark days," you may recognize is a line of Virgil's but with the two words "Phebe" and "Trojae" changed.[53] And I also, taking the words "father of humanity" and "redeemer" scarcely altered from a poem of Horace, applied them more meaningfully to Christ. And if only I had written more verse of this kind! But immersed as a youth in secular studies, I was overcome by an enormous and frenzied love of the poets. I could not live a day without Virgil. I composed several verses each day in imitation of him. Vittorino hoped I would become, as it were, another Virgil. There was at that time a boy, Ludovico da Feltre, of wonderful talent, whom Vittorino treated like a son, and who burned like me with the same passion [for poetry]. This boy I loved dutifully, but I wanted to excel him in other studies, and I envied him his ability in verse. For though I was more skilled at invention, he, though he could invent little and that with difficulty, could write more elegantly. Therefore, though I understood that, thus gifted, he had bested me, yet I would not confess it. And since with my kind of pride I could not tolerate second place, I applied my pen to other kinds of poetry. I wrote the tragedy *Progne* in my eighteenth year, and after I had written it, there was nothing Vittorino did not hope from me. As he read it tears poured from his eyes. I also wrote, while I was still at Mantua, a book on the education and training of boys, in satirical style. Thereafter, as my attention wandered in different directions, [I wrote] six satires and a lyric poem to Pope Martin V of blessed memory, at whose urging I undertook the clerical life.[54] But after that, my attention was taken up by ecclesiastical matters, and though I read much, I could write little. So now returning finally after fourteen years from the storms of the Roman Curia, and gathering up my spiritual energies [strewn about] like shipwrecked merchandise, I shall proceed to collect the capital with interest and repair the losses of past time. Why do I speak at such length about myself? So that you may understand that I have passed through the thorns and brambles of secular letters, from which I now dissuade you with such concern, and from which, having barely escaped with rent shirt and full of wounds, I flee to the healing powers of divine studies.

You also, Cecilia, virgin of Christ, must seek the Lord through the meadows of Scripture. For he says: "I am the flower of the field and the lily of the valleys."[55] Lift your eyes to the mountains, from where your help comes.[56] Do not seek him bloodless in the tomb. He ascends to heaven, he sits on the right hand of God the Father. There he should be sought, there, as much as possible, possessed by your mind, "for where thy treasure is, there also will thy heart be."[57] When this life has reached its end, may he rejoicing welcome you to the heavenly home, as he said: "Where I am, there also shall my servant be."[58] If he shall so receive a minister, how much more a spouse? Love him, therefore, with all your heart and with all your soul, seek him, rest in him. Meditate on his law day and night, seek his face always. Then with holy body and spirit strive to come to him so that, recognizing his spouse in her nuptial dress, he will invite you to the heavenly table with the choirs of holy virgins who have by their virginity deserved to be the companions of the immaculate Lamb.

What little I possess, excellent virgin, from the poverty of my studies, I am the first to offer you. There will be others whose minds labor for the church's treasury, who may perhaps by my example celebrate your name and write to you in richer abundance, as if to the Demetrias of our age.[59] Farewell in the Lord, and if anything in this letter pleases you, repay me with prayers. Florence, August 5.

## 18

*Francesco Barbaro to his Daughter Costanza*

## Introduction

Francesco Barbaro (1390–1454), trained as a humanist by a number of the prominent teachers of his day (Conversini, Barzizza, Guarino), was a major Venetian statesman. His humanism, like that of his daughter Costanza, was formed in his youth.[1] Among his four daughters, at least Costanza, his favorite, received a classical education. Three of them, and first of all Costanza, decided to enter a convent. It is as a member of the Convent of the Angels that Costanza receives this letter from her father in 1447.

The letter is one of consolation (a genre frequently employed by humanists) on the death of Costanza's cousin Luchina. (Many of the women represented in this anthology also wrote consolatory epistles to friends or relatives). The tone of the letter is morbid. Francesco dwells on details of physical decay and spiritual exaltation, mixed with the widespread humanist attitude of Stoic acceptance. This particular kind of pietism often appears in Venetian and Northern Italian humanism, though it may be even more heightened here than usual because addressed to a woman. That her father expects her to behave stoically speaks well of Costanza and of his opinion of her. As a formal Latin epistle, the letter suggests that their humanism was a strong bond between father and daughter. It is sprinkled throughout with references to both classical and Christian antiquity.

This translation is based on the Latin text in A. M. Querini, ed., *Francisci Barbari et aliorum ad ipsum epistolae* (Brescia, 1743), pp. 127–33.

## Text

I BELIEVE, DEAR COSTANZA, you have heard that Luchina Miani, in Padua, after a long and serious illness, departed from this fragile and vulnerable life in such a way that her death gave assurance of her salvation. Concerning her merits I could say much, if obligations and time permitted. And perhaps it is better to be silent than to say little, if it were not for the fact that recalling her virtue can ease and mollify our daily desire to see her. For although at times my eyes fill with tears, and the wound that reason should heal remembrance reopens, yet I feel pleasure in sorrow that she lived a life of such holiness that while she was still in the body she rose beyond it. It moves me that I, in my absence, am speaking with you about her—she with whom I cannot speak. Thus we are embracing in memory her whom we cannot embrace in body.

But I shall not presume, as would perhaps be allowed, to make up a speech in praise of her according to the custom and precedent of our ancestors; nor should I be faulted if in the matter of adorning and glorifying [my] daughter I think more about what I should than what I could do, especially since from my youth I have determined to seek models of counsel and behavior from the deeds of outstanding men. Thus Q. Fabius Maximus, a man illustrious in war and peace, and G. Caesar praised from the pulpit their dead sons, and the tears of the Roman populace, we read, did not shake their composure.[2] We have also learned through our fathers' memory that Robert, King of Sicily, did the same, which we both admire and praise.[3] I say nothing of Caesar who, when he heard, as he marched through Britain, of the death of his daughter, quickly, as he says, conquered sorrow, just as he was accustomed [to conquer] all things.[4] Books, antiquity, history, sparkle with examples as numerous as the stars, of those whose virtue was no less in facing the death of their loved ones than in bearing arms. But why do I look to antiquity? Our glorious prince Francesco Foscari, and the famous and brilliant citizen Federico Contarini, among others about whom I say nothing, so bore the death of their children that the one within three days spoke for the Republic wisely and eloquently in the Senate, and the other, when the death of his very gifted son was announced, managed somehow to put away his sorrow with dry eyes.[5]

But I am not asking you to do what they did, which you willingly do [in any case] – assuage your sorrow with reason – for though she was a worthy sister to you, you also knew that she was mortal, and you are now longing for her as though she were absent, not dead, so that you seem to await her, not to have lost her. For the disciples of Christ, as Jerome holds, should do better than the philosophers of the world.[6] And yet, peoples who did not know God and did not hope for resurrection, have so bravely and firmly borne the death of sons that they can provide a great example to Christians of the truth that the death of good men should be little mourned.[7] Both your name and your duty to your convent, if I may say so, require that you preserve with dignity a grave manner. You are not unaware what the Holy Bishop Lorenzo Giustiniani, our Father, did when those noble and great men, Marco and Leonardo, his brothers, died.[8] For at that time he had the glory of a soul so composed and moderate that all wondered whether he was alive, inasmuch as he was either unwilling to groan and complain, or, with his matchless piety, was unable to cry and sigh. You have also other domestic examples of virtue. Ermolao Barbaro, your brother, the Bishop of Treviso, so moderately and wisely bore the death of his sister that he grieved neither more nor less than the point at which it was right to cease, showing a piety neither superfluous nor deficient.[9] These men, therefore, as in the instance of their other merits, so also in this instance, you should and can imitate with all your power. For you cannot stem the tears of others unless you restrain your own. Also you know that because God is our aid – as we see in the case of Job – we can be injured but not vanquished.[10] Wherefore, I hope you will so govern your emotions that you will show neither less grief than love for your sister demands nor more than could be approved by the saints.

My consolation, then, you do not need, since you so speak with God and God himself with you, that there is no need to console you with words of human wisdom. And just as not to feel grief is inappropriate to a human being, likewise not to endure it is inappropriate to a wise human being. Wherefore, since nothing under the sun is perpetual and few things are long-lived, since, because they perish, all things cease to be, and since, finally, the law of nature cannot be changed and destruction is common to all, we must bear with composure what has befallen us. For we have not lost Luchina, but she whom we had we still have, and we should not imagine that we shall be here with her forever, as we know. Since things stand thus, I know that you do not expect from me medicine and solace for sorrow, not because my weak and arid mind, if I had books here with me, could not be richly watered from the fountain of Scripture, but because what can be said you already know, and because one better teaches endurance by example than by words.

But then you say: "Why do you not add lustre to Luchina's virtues by writing about them? Why do you not commend them to posterity? If you do not assuage my longing for her by consoling me, why do you write to me? It would be pious to do the former, wise and dutiful to do the latter, and it would bring you considerable praise." But the reasons I gave earlier, I think, satisfactorily answer both questions. I hope you will approve of what I decided, since I had to take into account your virtue and nature and my own moderation.

But I should not pass by in silence those things which excellent and honest women heard and saw a little before and after our Luchina departed to a better life. And don't think I am inventing or pretending, but, as Jerome said, I am a Christian man telling the truth about a Christian woman, so that the remembrance of her virtue does not console but arouses you to living well. Therefore I omit the fact that Luchina had a long while before been wholly converted to the Lord and had surrendered affectation of dress as well as her soul. In no way was anyone more merciful than she, or more kind towards the humble and poor. But what am I doing? Where am I going? About her life there should be silence, about her death speech. When, with the length and force of the sickness, the little strength she had was nearly consumed, she neither deceived her loved ones nor permitted herself to be deceived by vain hope, always knowing she would die. So moderately and wisely did she bear her fate — or rather, ours — and so much did she gain in spiritual strength while her members were dying that, her faith unshaken, she deserved for her long suffering a martyr's crown. In her, as it is written, sickness revealed how much value there was in health. And though no part of her body was free of pain, such was her endurance that with a spirit of mildness and gentleness she always defied the gravity of the sickness with a cheerful face. For she said, and nearly always had this on her tongue, great is the mercy of our God who wounds that he may heal us, who kills lest we die, and who in wondrous ways calls us to himself, so that the affliction of the body may be the material of our rewards. Thus, Abraham is tested in his son and is found faithful.[11] Joseph is sold that he may feed his father.[12] Ezekiel is threatened with death so that his life may be preserved.[13] Peter is terrified by the Lord's passion so that he may be made the prince of the apostles.[14] Paul is blinded so that he may see.[15] Who understands the intention of the Lord,[16] or who could counsel him?[17] What man is wise enough to understand this? What man is intelligent enough to know these things?

Luchina's husband, Francesco Miani, who, without her, it seemed, either wished to die or was unable to live, as well as others who were present there, she so bravely consoled that she showed that virtue should be measured not by sex but by loftiness of soul. She only complained about her discomfort when [her pain] was intense and [then she spoke] with restraint. Of her children and other dear ones she so spoke, looking up into heaven, that she overcame her love for the children by her greater love of God, and she forgot that she was a mother, as it is written, in order to remember that she was the handmaiden of Christ. The lesson of her death then was: "Be unwilling to love the world and those things in the world, but give a gift, and hope in the Lord."[18]

What need is there of more? Even before she had despaired of her life she put aside womanly softness, so composed her soul, and so spoke of God with mixed joy and tears that one could perceive that she did not fear death but piously hoped for it. Then, kneeling on the bare floor while imminent death shook her trembling limbs and tears flowed down her face, she received the sacraments of the church, bowing in humility as if she had always despised the world and longed for the convent. The day will escape me if I try to describe her patient [suffering] and superhuman faith. Without surcease the force of the sickness so tormented her and tortured her limbs and flesh that she was forced to live, it seemed, who was already dead. She could neither lie still nor stand, and she thrashed around the entire bed with her pain. "If I had a hundred tongues, a hundred mouths, and a voice of iron, I could not run through all the names of the punishments."[19] What more? All that we say is less than her sufferings, which she so bravely endured that she must never have been separated from heaven and from the mercy of God.

I am ashamed now and confess my error, because I have not described her illness, about which I should not have been reticent inasmuch as it would make the sanctity of her death appear even greater. I decided to be silent, however, lest its shamefulness, the indecency of the language [needed to describe it] and to even touch on the [diseased] part [of her body], should offend your chaste ears and summon your thoughts from heaven to earth, making dust and pity of our glory. For it is improper to reveal [in words] — for the same reason that we veil our eyes — the secret parts of the body. Moreover, frequent bleeding and the experiments of the doctors had ulcerated and lacerated her members, producing such filth and fetor that there was scarcely anyone who could bear her daily martyrdom and rotting wounds. I would have passed all this by in silence if it had not been demonstrated in the corpse how much remarkable endurance she had in life, for soon after death the decay seemed transformed into an odor of sweetness.

Permit me to share with you what that excellent woman Regina Barbaro (who nearly always was present and closed Luchina's eyes) affirmed, and Regina's testimony carries great weight with everyone because of her faith, religion, and wisdom. The same thing is reported by others, among them the woman Giustina, if I do not mistake the name, who had lived many years in honorable widowhood and never left Luchina's side. [Giustina reports that] when [Luchina] was so exhausted and stunned by sickness that while still alive she seemed to be the ghost of a breathing corpse and was unbelievably deformed (though before her sickness she had been lovely and her body possessed of much grace), after she fell asleep in the Lord there was no pallor, no ugliness in her face, no gauntness or meanness or horror in the lineaments of her mouth. Rather had her face acquired a certain grace and a not unpleasing seriousness, so that she looked lovely and not ugly, and one would have thought her asleep and not dead. Moreover, without the help of any medical art all the wounds of her body were so suddenly healed that only scars could be seen, and in place of fetor such a sweet fragrance followed that both indoors and out it was perceived and admired. Nor did it cease before her corpse had been brought to Venice and piously and with splendor laid in the sepulchre of her ancestors. Those present were so affected that not a single one of them believed what he saw.

Some signs also appeared to us which I think it wiser not to write about. Whoever can understand them, let him understand.[20] I, however, infer that our Luchina, after a life well-lived, either had come or shortly will come to that grade of happiness that only the holy enjoy, both because faithfully, while scarcely still in the flesh, she seemed to live beyond the flesh, and because after a long martyrdom her devout spirit brought it about that her lacerated and ulcerated body was suddenly cleansed and glorified after her death (all due to her cleanness of soul). Thus, the nobility of her mind was clothed, so to speak, in splendid garb.

Since things stand thus, beloved Costanza, we should not begrudge Luchina's glory but rather rejoice that she lived and died in such a way that there can be no doubt that she moved to a better life. We may censure ourselves if, in the meantime, we do not conquer by reason the sorrow that time will soften. Let us balance against the brief span of this life eternal memory and so compose ourselves that we learn to live by dying well and to die by living well. And let us rejoice to care as much for the dead as they do for us. Farewell. May he who watches over Israel preserve you in body and spirit. To your Mother Superior, who is the head of the convent, and to the virgins who serve God together with you, commend me, and aid me with your prayers. November 30, [1447]

## 19

*Lauro Quirini sends greetings
to the most noble and most eloquent virgin
Isotta Nogarola*

## Introduction

This is the first of two letters translated in this anthology written to Isotta Nogarola by male humanist admirers. It was also the first in point of time, being composed sometime between 1443 and 1448.

The writer, Lauro Quirini (1420–1480/81), was born into a patrician Venetian family and studied at Padua where he took his arts degree in 1440 and his law degree in 1448.[1] After completing the latter he returned to Venice in 1449 where, apparently on his own initiative, he lectured publicly on Aristotle's *Ethics*. In 1451 and 1452 he lectured on rhetoric and moral philosophy — subjects of particular interest to humanists — at Padua. Thereafter he returned to his native Candia (Crete) where he remained for the rest of his life. He belonged to the inner circle of Venetian humanists, writing on a number of characteristic humanist themes.

This letter stands in striking contrast to the one which follows it, addressed also to Nogarola, but from another admirer. Quirini says nothing at all about Nogarola's virginity or her rejection of the life of the world. He speaks only about the life of learning. In so doing, he addresses her as he might address a male humanist. Indeed, he appears to treat her as one, for he says to her near the beginning of the letter that she has overcome her own nature. "For that true virtue which is proper to men you have pursued with remarkable zeal." He can address Nogarola as if she were a man because, in pursuing her studies, she has "overcome" her sex, i.e., ceased to be a woman and become a man. She is, of course, compared favorably to learned women of the past and even likened to Hypatia, the Neoplatonist philosopher, pride of the school of Alexandria, under whom a number of men (including Synesius, mentioned in this letter) studied.

The program of study that he recommends to her extends beyond humanist disciplines to the philosophical concerns central to the arts curriculum of the Renaissance Italian university. He advises her to read Aristotle, held in high regard in Padua, and those commentaries on Aristotle available to her in Latin by Boethius and the Arab philosophers Avicenna, Averroes, and Al Ghazali.[2] He omits the ancient Greek commentators who are unavailable to her because of her ignorance of Greek, expressing at the same time the hope that they may soon be translated into Latin. He warns her against recent commentators, i.e., medieval interpretations of Aristotle. Only Thomas Aquinas, among medieval philosophers and theologians, is mentioned with approval. Quirini shares the humanist prejudice, stemming from Petrarch, that medieval interpretations of Aristotle distorted his meaning. According to Bruni and other translators of Aristotle, they also distorted his eloquence, and humanist translations attempted to restore that eloquence—even if it could not be found in the text. Be that as it may, Quirini regards Aristotle as the fountain of philosophical wisdom. That is why he wants Nogarola to come into direct contact with Aristotle by reading his texts and those interpreters who elucidate rather than distort his meaning. His insistence on this shows the great respect Quirini has for Nogarola's mind.

This translation is based on the Latin text in Nogarola, *Opera*, ed. Abel, 2:9–22.

## Text

SOME SORT OF ALMOST boorish shyness,[3] remarkable Isotta, greatest glory of the women of our age, has restrained me to this day from writing to you, whom I have revered, though silently, yet certainly with much love. But now I have determined to be guided by that old proverb: "Fall once rather than hang forever." For when that excellent man Giovanni Dolfin came to Padua from Verona, and among the many notable monuments of the city showed me your letters already collected in a volume, and I read them with great pleasure, I could only rejoice greatly and expressly congratulate you. But your brother Leonardo, a youth of excellent mind, now pursuing diligently with most worthy labor the best philosophy, also asked me a long time ago now to write something to you, for since at this time you are seriously studying, as he said, dialectic and philosophy, he wished that I myself advise you reliably and amicably about which masters in particular you should follow in these higher disciplines. Several other friends also exhorted me to write to you. But the glorious and honorable fame which you have already deservedly enjoyed for a long time compels me—even if I were unwilling—to revere you and to compose this letter for you. I hope you will accept and recognize it as coming from a friend who has the most kindly wishes.

This letter asks of you nothing else than that you pursue in the most splendid way, until death, that same course of right living which you have followed since childhood. But if you find this letter dry and uncultivated, forgive me. For at this time we are especially interested in that philosophy which does not value an ornamented style.[4] Therefore, let your delicate ears put up with sometimes dry figures of speech, I beg you. For you who have been trained in the polished and exquisite art of rhetoric and are accustomed to elegant discourses and melodious style, rightly can demand the most ornate eloquence; but we semi-orators and petty philosophers are content for the most part with little eloquence, and that clumsy. Wherefore I rejoice for you and offer congratulations for your virtue. And should we not greatly rejoice that you can be named among those admittedly few but certainly famous women [of the past], when we see that the ancients gloried in the learning of such outstanding women? And indeed, may I say, let us at this time pass by in silence the women both of Greece and of Rome, among whom were most notably the Sibyls,[5] Aspasia, the teacher of the great Pericles,[6] Sappho,[7] Proba who wrote the *Cento*,[8] Amesia,[9] Hortensia,[10] Cornelia, the mother of the Gracchi,[11] who were learned only in the arts of poetry and rhetoric and whose fame was widespread. It will be sufficient to look at one. Synesius, a distinguished philosopher, had as his teacher Hypatia, whom he exalted with such praise and such declarations as to demonstrate that all the philosophers of that time enthusiastically admired her.[12] Rightly, therefore, should you also, famous Isotta, receive the highest praises, since you have indeed, if I may so speak, overcome your own nature. For that true virtue which is proper to men you have pursued with remarkable zeal—not the mediocre virtue which many men seek, but that which would befit a man of the most flawless and perfect wisdom. Thus Cicero rightly said: "You young men have a womanly spirit, but that girl has a man's spirit."[13] Therefore, dissatisfied with the lesser studies, you have applied your noble mind also to the higher disciplines, in which there is need for keenness of intelligence and mind. For you are engaged in the art of dialectic, which shows the way for learning the truth. Having mastered it you may become engaged skillfully and knowledgeably in a still more splendid and fertile field of philosophy [metaphysics]. Therefore, just like a teacher challenged by the sight of a warm and indeed loyal personality, I shall teach you, venerable virgin.

I want, therefore, my Isotta, because of the fineness of your mind in which I take great pleasure and the familiarity resulting from our correspondence, to address you as though I were your brother and to demand as my right that you not only avoid and shun these new philosophers and dialecticians as men without knowledge of true philosophy and dialectic, but also that you spurn all their writings. For when they teach dialectic they do not follow the long proven method of this ancient discipline, but they introduce I do not know what kinds of childish sophisms, inextricable arguments, and unnecessary digressions, and thus obfuscate the clear and distinct order of this discipline. In order to appear to know much, they distort everything, even the most obvious, with a kind of futile subtlety and, as the comic writer says, they "look for knots in a bulrush."[14] For this reason, tied up in these complexities, they cannot aspire to true and solid philosophy. And so in that field also, while they want to be seen as perceptive debators, they wrestle too much with the truth, as the old saying goes,[15] and so have lost it. For just as dull-witted negligence gives birth to heedless ignorance, so over-precise investigation cannot satisfactorily discover certain truth, as Labeo's opinion in civil law elegantly states.[16] But on account of all their elaborate argumentation they are judged to be both subtle philosophers and perceptive debators, and even though true science is concerned with being, these sophists pertinaciously and contentiously quarrel about non-being. [Referring to such as these] Aristotle declared that they do not dispute but chatter,[17] with the result that the mind can scarcely—and a well-trained mind cannot at all—understand them. There is also an additional important reason for their ignorance: the texts of Aristotle, which contain true and elegant philosophy, some neglect from ignorance, whereas others, greedy for glory and ambitious for honor, while they do not at all understand this most profound and deep of philosophers, yet they rashly set about [writing] commentaries. And so in trying to divide the divine Aristotle subtly [into topics for their expositions], they mutilate him instead, in elucidating they obscure him, in uncovering [his meaning] they bury it. Now that I have hooted these men off the stage, I shall briefly teach whom you should follow.

Read studiously the glorious monuments of Boethius Severinus, unquestionably a most intelligent and abundantly learned man.[18] Read all the treatises he learnedly composed on the dialectical art and the commentaries he wrote on Aristotle's *Categories* and his twofold work on Aristotle's *On Interpretation*, the first following the literal sense, the second according to the understanding of a higher sort.[19] In these you will be able to examine the views of nearly all the most reliable Greek commentators. I marvel enormously at the mortals of our time who abandon a man so learned, so excellent, so eminent in the disciplines of the good arts, and I don't know whom . . . but it is better to be silent, lest I incite against me the vulgar crowd of philosophers who may imagine that I am plotting against them in this letter. But after you have mastered dialectic, which is the method of knowing, you should read diligently and carefully the moral books of Aristotle, which he writes divinely, in which you may unfailingly recognize the essence of true and solid virtue.[20] And if you also, as you should, act upon his excellent teaching in your life, he will lead you as no one else can to the height and extremity of the good. But after you have also digested this part of philosophy, which is concerned with human matters, with a certain nobility of soul you should also set out for that ample and vast other part, which is threefold.[21] [Here] you should begin especially with those disciplines which we call by the Greek name mathematics, which offer knowledge of such certainty (even though it is very difficult) that many philosophers, and these the most serious, think that we can know nothing with certainty unless mathematicians have demonstrated it. Afterwards, strive unceasingly and determinedly to pursue that philosophy which we call natural, in which we are taught about sensible things and those having continuous motion. But finally, you should engage yourself in metaphysics, which our Peripatetics call a divine science, so that you may be able to know God and the three substances. This is the right path and famous order of truth which caused the ancient philosophers who observed it to arrive, as we see, at such a degree of excellence that we do not hesitate to call them divine.

Then if you had knowledge of Greek letters, I would teach you whom you should follow, who would lead you to the peak of all things. But since you lack only this—though certainly a great advantage—pay no attention to these modern Latin philosophers whom we discussed a little earlier, who deal in the debris of philosophy, but diligently and carefully follow the Arabs who very nearly approach the Greeks. Averroes, indeed, a barbarous and uncultivated man, but otherwise an exceptional philosopher and rare judge of things, you should always and continually read.[22] Even though on your first reading you will perhaps despair of understanding him, yet if you work hard you will find him easy. But if you wish quickly to understand the Philosopher, then read Thomas Aquinas often, who provides as it were the entryway to the understanding of Aristotle and Averroes.[23] But though you may touch lightly on the Commentator, reject all the others. Thus you should frequently read not only his commentaries and treatises, but also Avicenna on natural philosophy and the *Summa* of Al Ghazali.[24] These Arabs will be able to train you in the true discipline of the Peripatetics until we have sufficient leisure and opportunity to translate the Aristotelian works into Latin, and to compose commentaries and arrange into a simpler system those things which Aristotle wrote plainly, explaining and unravelling his majestic phrases and involved obscurities. [24a]

You should also make use of those studies which you have splendidly embraced from your youth, particularly history, for history is as it were the teacher of life,[25] somehow making ours the wisdom of the ancients, inflaming us to imitate great men. For why did our ancestors study history so zealously unless they thought it to be nothing other than the example of a good and holy life? Historians have preserved for us every trace left by antiquity. But Cicero I pass by in silence, on whom one should constantly feed. Often have I been tired, but never satiated, when I have laid him down.

It remains for me to exhort you to the performance of virtue and to the excellent studies of letters. But since I realize that you are inflamed to both of these with a certain wondrous desire, I may close this letter once I have said one last thing. I regret very much, my beautiful Isotta, born of Apollo, raised by the divine Mercury on nectar, and taught by holy Muses,[26] sorrowfully, sorrowfully I say I grieve that we have lost the fruits of a long acquaintance. We must strive, amid a multitude of responsibilities, to be able in some way to recover that lost pleasure. I promise you, therefore, with Attic faith[27] – in the event you would not believe me without this vow – by wind and earth I swear to you that I preserve your sweet memory within the secret places of my heart.

These things, goddess Isotta, of great virtue and honesty, I have freely written, moved by conscience, by duty, and by that marvelous affection I feel towards you, which affection, once I know that you have accepted it gladly and willingly, I shall maintain as long as you wish. Love, indeed, longs for a beloved. Therefore, you should love Lauro,[28] among many other reasons particularly for this, that it is always green, for which reason the pagans consecrated it to Apollo, your god of wisdom. But we will exchange more jests at another time when it suits us both, with honest wit. Take care of yourself so that you may be well, and study so that you may be wise and nobly imitate Hippolytus, considering philosophy your delight and the center of all else that you love.[29] For nothing is more lovely than philosophy, nothing more beautiful, nothing more lovable, as our Cicero said.[30] But I [shall add], perhaps more truly, that there is nothing among human things more divine than philosophy. For this is the one most holy discipline which teaches true wisdom and instructs in the right mode of living. Those, consequently, who are ignorant of philosophy go through life not only having achieved no good but even having committed evil. Accordingly, give your whole heart, as they say,[31] to philosophy alone, for I want you to be not semi-learned, but to have knowledge of all the good arts, that is, to know the art of good speaking and the discipline of correct disputation, as well as the science of human and divine things. Farewell, and I entreat you, love me. At Padua.

20

*Ludovico Foscarini to Isotta Nogarola*

## Introduction

Ludovico Foscarini we have already encountered in selection 10 as the interlocutor with Isotta Nogarola in the dialogue on Adam and Eve. This letter was written during the same period as the correspondence leading to the composition of the dialogue (1453).

The letter is somewhat redundant, but all the more revealing for that. Like Correr writing to Cecilia Gonzaga, Foscarini dwells most on the fact that Nogarola has renounced the world. The sentiment is not very different from that of Correr writing to a woman who intended to take religious vows. Nogarola's virginity is referred to more than her learning. Her character, as mentioned earlier, had been scurrilously attacked by an anonymous Veronese writer in 1438. Foscarini makes it a point to emphasize that Nogarola's character is above reproach. The emphasis placed on these themes makes it clear that they were the points of uneasiness in her culture — especially for a woman who had chosen a career of learning without marriage and without taking religious vows.

At the same time, Foscarini praises Nogarola's learning as beyond that of many learned men. He praises the fine qualities of her mind without overstatement. But notice that the most remarkable quality about her mind is that it resides in the body of a woman. She has achieved something rare for one of her sex, so that she is more to be admired than a man. This is, in fact, not an unfair judgment. Given the obstacles which Nogarola had to overcome in order to accomplish what she did, she was indeed rare.

This translation is based on the Latin text in Nogarola, *Opera*, ed. Abel, 2:39–51.

## Text

Y OU PRAISE, MOST WORTHY VIRGIN, my devotion in admiring your virtues which very nearly approach the divinity of the heavens, but I wonder at and detest those who do not have a high regard for them. If the worthiest matrons of our time will allow me to say this, you, excelling all in my judgment, have overcome your nature first of all by your obedience to your saintly mother, from whom the habits of your most holy life took their first beginnings. Her you hear, her judgment you never dispute, whatever she commands and ordains you believe to be fruitful, and you consider it sufficient authority if there is something your pious mother wishes. Ready always in soul, mind, body, you obey her will . . . ,[1] and your other near ones you have with such affability embraced that they are most happy who can for a while linger with you. All desires you have crushed in seed, you have con-

demned the lush wealth which even by many wise men often was more highly regarded than was proper, you were taught by the laws of Lycurgus who
prohibited the Spartans from using gold and silver, believing by that edict that
he had extirpated the root of all crimes.[2] You have chosen not a necessary
but a voluntary poverty. Besides food and the most urgent necessities, nothing
at all have you taken from your most ample patrimony. I see the golden robes
of your family, their full wardrobes and frequent changes, while you always
wear the same dress, neither dirty nor ornate, which brings you closer to your
creator. Devoted to Christian thoughts, you disdain both our public and our
private responsibilities. You have renounced pleasure and shunned delights,
you constantly attend to learning and prayer, nothing beyond Christ do you
desire. You are most wealthy in poverty, and those riches, I say, in which
Epicurus correctly taught all to be rich, saying: "If you wish to make a man
rich, do not add money but subtract desire."[3] Since, then, you do not desire
gold, nor seek it nor pursue it nor in prayer beg for it, since you need little
and are content with little, you are leading your life without anxiety, richer
than any queen. Though situated on earth, you model yourself on angels, saying or thinking nothing unless it pertains to the praise of God. Dress, word,
gesture, mind and works are in concord, [and at death] you will fly to heaven
light and unclothed, unburdened by the weight of wealth or sins.

Given the fame of your family—which in a continuous succession [of genera-
tions] has been supplied and adorned with great-spirited men and worthy
matrons—and your outstanding fortune, possessions, and appearance, you could
have chosen from all Italy a husband at will. For if all your famous sisters—to
whom in no respect are you inferior—became worthy of illustrious marriages,
what can we think would have happened to you, in whom shine the outstanding and rare gifts of all past, present, and future women? . . .[4] Oh more happy
mode of life! You have devoted all that you are to sanctity. Only religion is
stable; it is not lost, it does not change. Amid the great and turbulent storms
and wretched calamities of the city, the earth, the times, it maintains you
pleasantly in the quietest province of the mind—since all things prosperous,
peaceful, and welcome, occur to those loving the Lord, all those adverse, wretched and bitter to those spurning him. For though the counsels of the evil may
for the moment admittedly appear attractive, it is always better to act upon
those of the good, not according to the poets' songs, but by the judgment of
wise men. Here is your most admirable and incredible humanity, by which
you yield to all, although you surpass all in virtue. I shall remain silent about
virginity, concerning the excellence of which the books of holy men are full.
I say nothing of your modesty, temperance, and other glories, which in the
judgment of the best men are numbered as virtues. Because you are unique,
unique honors are owed to you.

Having been given to us by the highest God, raised by a wise mother, you seem to have been born to all types of the greatest virtues which all have been instilled in you, you may believe, as a gift of God rather than by the generosity of nature, for this reason above all, because you never insist on your own glory; and yet, however much you scorn praise, that much more intensely it is offered to you. You follow Christ, you have offered yourself as a purest living sacrifice and pleasing to God.[5] Your serious demeanor, your judgment seem beyond your years and sex. An enemy of idleness, you have never failed yourself, nor religion, nor learning. By adding and heaping virtue on virtue, you have employed all the diligence of the greediest merchants in your business of letters and Christian life. You lead your life and spirit amid hard work and long hours devoted to study, desire you do not understand, pleasures you do not recognize, luxury you take no delight in. You do not know what it is like to stroll through your noble city. From no literary labor do you seek respite, amid no vigils do you seek sleep. Pastimes, applause, which many women avidly pursue, you do not even take the time to think of. From heaven—to which we confidently predict you will have a most easy entry—you have indeed fallen. And since you understand rightly that goodness derives from and is adorned by learning, as much time as virgins of your age give to arranging their faces you give to your divine soul in the cultivation of the liberal arts in studies. And you do well. Moses did not turn to holy contemplation until he had trained his mind in [studious] disciplines.[6] Daniel first was educated among the Babylonians in the doctrine of the Chaldaeans before he advanced to divine things.[7] When Geno asked how he could best live, Apollo advised him with a famous reply: by revering the dead.[8] Heeding such admonitions, you have always wisely been engaged in letters, in those . . . which,[9] I say, render you learned and good. And though you heard the poets in your youth from learned teachers, you have wished . . . to master those disciplines by which your soul can best be nourished; and more zealously than the Epicureans were said to have pursued the delights of the body you were delighted by rhetoric, in which you greatly excel. . . . Thereafter you turned to sacred volumes. Not with a superficial learning, but by diligent and acute study, you have omitted nothing at all that you knew pertained to the best mode of leading the present life and to future glory. And although you have read and understood much, I believe you have [acquired] most by sacred prayers from the Holy Spirit. For otherwise you could not feel so deeply, speak so elegantly, write so richly, with the admiration of all.

I often peruse the histories of the most outstanding women. Ancient Rome, which extended its empire to the ends of the earth and its spirit as high as Olympus, produced none equal to you.[10] Your writings from as long ago as your adolescence and an even younger age exist, which manifest a rare mind

and not ordinary knowledge. When I am in your presence and hear you speaking, I recognize such maturity of counsel, such unique prudence, such dignified
instruction, that to me it seems in no way possible that such things proceed
from acuity of mind alone and wide reading, but from that Holy Spirit which
blows where it will.[11] Having taken into its service your body, which has been
by no stain of pleasure soiled, most splendid in virginity, adorned not in dress
but in morals, the Holy Spirit governs you, inspires the tongue and other functions of all your members with worthiest affects, and permits nothing about
you to be fabricated, nothing suspected, even by the evil. . . .[12] [And] you in
soul, mind, and sense transformed in the Holy Spirit, do not live, but it lives
in you. The ancient learned men who sang songs to Sempronia and Cornificia[13]
would have extolled you to heaven with praise, since you have rendered poetry and every kind of human study in speaking and disputing most familiar
to you. Equipped to read sweetly and write easily in all the liberal disciplines,
you surpass learned men in pronunciation, bookish men in celerity and elegance.
I have often seen you, as you know, speak extemporaneously with such glory
that I suspect there was nothing ever more worthy and sweet. What can be
more glorious, what more magnificent, than to hear you pleading in a way
most worthy of majesty, gracious with noble modesty, bright with distinction, severe with authority, in teaching dignified and in diligence most sound?
What woman therefore was ever more learned than you or could be, who
from the school of childhood up to this age, by learning and by teaching, have
committed to memory more books than many learned men have seen? What
kind of liberal learning is there in which you are not versed? Oratory, poetry,
philosophy, theology declare that there is nothing that can adorn the mortal
mind which you have neglected.

   To you, therefore, I do not promise adequate praises. Those who erected
a bronze statue to Sappho, the girl from Lesbos,[14] should have erected it to
you, since in this age there is more wisdom in you than all women in all ages
even impudently could claim. I always except those whom our religion wor-
ships and whom we revere with pious prayers. Solomon, who praised the Queen
of Sheba, would have paid you a visit once he had espied the peculiar wisdom
of your noble family and had found out that you considered as delights, not
gold or embroidered robes, but Cicero, Virgil, Jerome, Augustine;[15] and he
would have judged you the most outstanding of all, who are nourished by
virtue and literary leisure, unconcerned with pleasures, and, unimpeded, follow
the highest good. Your Verona rejoices in her marble monuments, theatres,
basilicas, mountains, rivers, paintings, and, in short, in every most exquisite
ornament of the people. It admires your famous ancestors, venerates your noble brothers, reveres your prudent mother, with stupor gazes upon the incredible
beauty of your sisters, and triumphs in [you], the divine virgin as though its

true and matchless light, splendor, and ornament, for you are known to surpass ancient and modern forms of virtues. As many times as I bring you to
mind, I seem to see Catelina Crichastina and other most holy and learned
virgins.[16] The heretics who suspect that the histories of their virtues are false
will believe in religious books once they understand that you with constancy
and learning and every illustrious kind of virtue have in your time as much
exceeded them as they in their times are said to have excelled other women.
Normally, I love fine minds but refrain from frequent association with them.
But of you and with you I cannot be silent, since in Isotta, than whom none
is superior in virtue, that sex greatly pleases, a little burdened by the weakness
of other women. Even the worst men make so much of your religion and
learning that you are judged to have been born for the glory of our age.

I am forced, therefore, to love you—to return to the point from which I
have digressed at length—by certain reason and experience, because there is
no earthly body which has dwelling within it a soul of more brilliant virtue.
In saying this, I do not deceive nor am I deceived. Concerning no woman
have so many and such excellent judgments been published, there is no place
in Italy so deserted that the fame of your name has not reached it. When
with righteous . . . and confident soul you went to Rome for the purpose of
a pious pilgrimage, with what counsel, with what authority, with what rich
style did you speak, arousing the great admiration of the Pope and your
brothers![17] Great are those who among the great are esteemed as great. Here
let me say no more, nor propose other examples, since now both for me and
for all posterity you will always be a highest example. Nor will anyone doubt
how great you were, who already for a long time not by my writings, but
by your own merits, have been famed beyond the stars.[18] The letters of learned men which are delivered to you from various and diverse places have in-
creased your authority, and your responses are awaited and circulated more
avidly than once the counsels of the Sibyls. Cardinal [Giuliano] Cesarini judged
nothing more worthy in his whole long journey than meeting you, and concluded that nature, virtue, and learning were at your command.[19] For that
reason, you may rejoice in the Lord, since you so greatly excel by birth, are
outstanding in majesty, flourish in letters, are conspicuous in virtue—which
should be praised in every sex, but in a woman much more, because it rarely
occurs and thus is judged more worthy and more admirable. I would write
much more, if this discourse had been intended to undertake all those matters
which the magnitude of your merits deserves. But since I accidentally embarked
on this speech because I wished to praise you, you may not accept the things
I have said, since . . . to enumerate your matchless virtues would require several
volumes and an age of talk.[20] Farewell.

21

### Fra Tommaso of Milan, Order of Preachers, to Silvestro Cereta, Father of Laura Cereta

## Introduction

Fra Tommaso of Milan and Silvestro Cereta were perhaps the two most significant men in Laura Cereta's intellectual life. Silvestro, her father, was her teacher, perhaps her only teacher, and the chief male supporter of her work. We see from this letter that he — no doubt proud of his daughter's accomplishments — sent some of her letters to Fra Tommaso, who is here responding to the gift. From this letter it becomes clear that Fra Tommaso was not Laura's teacher, as she refers to him in one of her letters to him, for he is only discovering her work for the first time. His education must have been humanist as well as scholastic, for he does not write medieval Latin, though he also does not write a fluid humanist Latin. His style is strange and his Latin difficult to decipher. He seems to hide his ideas behind his expression of them. For this reason the translations which follow in this and the next selection are freer than the other translations in this anthology.

As is evident in this letter, although Fra Tommaso admires Cereta's precocity, his interests are primarily religious, and he laments the fact that she does not have religious models to follow. This is important for the subsequent correspondence between Cereta and Fra Tommaso, as we shall see in the next selection.

This translation is based on the text published by A. Rabil, Jr., *Laura Cereta: Quattrocento Humanist* (Binghamton, 1981), part 3, no. 9, pp. 143–47.

## Text

BOTH THE MISER and the liberal and generous person desire wealth. The miser stores it away to be consumed by rust and worms, while the generous person distributes it to everyone. I confess, Silvestro, that you have made me drunk with the riches you have bestowed on me. But I find such lack of satisfaction in them that no supply, however great, could match the desire you have aroused in me. I am like one who has unexpectedly grasped what he has most wanted for a long time, but I know that it is not enough for me, since something newer is always oozing sweetly from that milky fountain. Do not think me a miser on this account, for things I desire greatly can never grow faint or old.

Thus it is with very great pleasure of mind that I have read the letters of Laura you sent me. I was especially impressed by her letter to Felix Tadinus[1] in which, with balanced style and inner meditation, she examines the necessity and causes of death. I liked her assertion that her grief was overcome more by reason than by weeping. And how beautifully she records that it was love rather than grief which inflicted her mortal wound. In her letter to Sigismundus de Buccis[2] how subtle the inventions, how severe the language, how eloquent and appropriate the words and endings which make her sentences sound beautiful. She is like a new Penelope, weaving garments skillfully with her nightly work.[3] She would be the envy of the Babylonian Lucretia and the Amazon Emily, one of whom pleased Frederick Augustus, the other the victor Theseus in his tent.[4] Skillfully also does she describe the clash with the Germans, the drawing up of the battle lines, the reinforcements, the battle at the Adige River near Brescia where both armies were destroyed.[5] What can I say about her funeral oration in honor of an ass,[6] the painted affectation of women,[7] the descriptions of the course of the heavens,[8] her knowledge of herbs,[9] her story of a journey to the underworld?[10] I confess that I was amazed. What has remained unknown to this girl? What has her fertile talent not uncovered or her diligence not traced down? What has nature kept hidden from her and what authors has she not read?

Made drunk by all these great letters, I thirst for still more of the precious liquid that may be squeezed from this strong wine-press. Send me more of her work. I hope I may ask without offending her. I am honored to have been introduced to a person of such incredible excellence.

And yet she gives herself to things unworthy of her. She is neither a Magdalene to Christ[11] nor a Dorcas to Peter[12] nor a Drusiana to John[13] nor a Paula or Eustochium to Jerome[14] nor a Scholastica to Benedict.[15] Oh, if she had been born in those times or some saint had been born later! But Christ does not walk among us today. There is no Ambrose, Macharius, Augustine, Anthony, or Jerome.[16] Nevertheless, if we read their works they will dwell with us. Indeed, they dwell with us in their works better than they dwelt with the women mentioned above in life. For in life they were capable of sin, but in their books they live only in our minds, purified of their weaknesses. Thus if we read them we can imitate them more truly. If Laura has been given such a talent as she has, she should use it to such a noble purpose as this rather than merely to buy flowers.

Please forgive me, and may Laura also indulge me. For I am consumed by zeal for God, by whom I trust Laura may also always be comforted. October 9, 1487.

22

*Fra Tommaso of Milan, Order of Preachers,*
*to Laura Cereta*

## Introduction

Six letters were exchanged between Cereta and Fra Tommaso, three by each correspondent. The first in point of time was written by Cereta on October 21, 1486. The letter appears in some respects to be a response to the letter of Fra Tommaso to Silvestro (preceding selection), for in it Laura refers to reading the works of Augustine and Jerome, to whom Fra Tommaso had referred at the end of his letter to Silvestro. On the other hand, the tone of that letter would hardly explain the letter translated here, which is dated November 4, 1487, for in this letter Fra Tommaso is quite upset over attacks directed at him by Cereta. We must therefore assume that the first letter written by Cereta, quite different in tone from the other five between the two correspondents, was written earlier, and that Fra Tommaso was a long-time acquaintance of the family (Laura's first letter was written one year before Silvestro sent some of his letters to Fra Tommaso). If this is true, however, we might wonder about Fra Tommaso's surprise at receiving subsequent letters written by Cereta.

In any case, the situation is quite different here. Cereta had been attacked by her critics, both male and female. Some of her responses, written both before and after this letter to Fra Tommaso, indicate that she was involved in defending her role as a learned woman. Somehow Fra Tommaso became involved – at least in Cereta's mind – with those attacking her. We have no sources to suggest just how this might have come about. Her second letter to him is stinging. All three of his letters to her, written in the short period between November 4 and December 12, 1487, complain of her biting criticism. The letter translated here, both the first and the shortest of the three, is nevertheless characteristic and sets up the conflict discussed in all three between the pride involved in writing learned letters and the humility demanded of a Christian. Cereta is too proud; she needs humility.

In her last letter to Fra Tommaso, dated February 4, 1488, Cereta gives in. She is going to take his advice, put down her pen, and live a more humble life. A few months after she wrote this letter she published her letters. Thereafter we hear from her no more.

This translation is based on the Latin text published by Rabil, *Laura Cereta*, part 3, no. 10, pp. 148–50.

## Text

YOUR LETTER WAS SAVAGE and sharp, but the letter of Bonifacio wounded me, though you cleverly tried to hide its sting. The apparent fragrance of your letter, however, concealed nettles and thickets underneath, like the honey bee which conceals its sting in an abundant flow of honey, striving to hide poison with salt. But the sweetness of its milk does not prevent the sting from penetrating with the sharpness of vinegar and burning the skin as if it were mustard.

Your [critical words, like a] dog prone to barking, has leaped on Master Benedict of the Order of Preachers like a foaming wild boar. You accuse him of preferring oratorical to natural or revealed wisdom. But underneath your attack on him is a concealed attack on me, whom you are too timid to attack openly. Feeling yourself wounded, you have attacked me with words of passion rather than reason.

You say that I, an uncouth and babbling man, approached you unsought. [Though perhaps not "uncouth,"] I have certainly avoided the pompous rhetoric of your letters. At the same time I studied oratory [through Seneca and Lucan rather than through Cicero][1] until I was fifteen years old, [but for the next seven years after that I turned my attention to moral philosophy.]

I do not see how you can accuse me of betrayal. What have I advised you that is so treacherous? You have put all kindness aside in attacking me. The fault lies in you for distorting the meaning of my letter. Can you not respond to what someone else has written except by attacking it? You act as if you were second to none in talent, sending your literary productions to all the educated people of the world, like a lioness who fears no one's approach. It is hypocrisy to claim humility but at the same time to seek to be exalted for your work. If, as you claim, you have humble thoughts about yourself, why are you driven to fury in such trivial matters by your admirers, but then accuse yourself more severely than they accuse you? You humble yourself to no purpose if you accuse yourself of something but then get angry when you hear the same thing from another person. Such behavior shows how much credit you expect to be given to your own voice.

And so, sister, take a deep breath. Unwrinkle your forehead. Prune the sting from your tongue. Blunt your pen and temper it with the file of modesty. Remember that laurel berries are an antidote to poison, inasmuch as the laurel and the oak dissolve poisons. Farewell in the Lord. November 4, 1487.

## 23

### Angelo Poliziano to Cassandra Fedele, a most learned Venetian Maiden: Encomium

## Introduction

Angelo Poliziano (1454–94) was one of the leading humanists in Florence, a member of the circle surrounding Lorenzo de' Medici. He mastered both Latin and Greek, studying in Florence–where he was sent from his native Montepulciano–under the best Greek masters. Marsilio Ficino and Pico della Mirandola, the two leading figures in the Platonic Academy of Florence, were his close friends. Indeed, his friendship with Pico, who is mentioned in this letter to Cassandra, is one of the dominant features of his letters. He began teaching grammar and rhetoric in Florence in 1480, lecturing on Quintilian, Suetonius, Homer, and Aristotle (the latter under the influence of Pico). He published his *Miscellanea*, minute philological discussions, under the prodding of Lorenzo de' Medici in 1489. His editions of the Greek authors Plutarch, Alexander of Aphrodisias and Epictetus were important and highly regarded in his day.[1]

This letter to Fedele was written in 1491, when Poliziano was at the height of his career (Lorenzo de' Medici was to die one year later; Poliziano survived him by only two years) and Fedele at the height of her renown. She was at the time twenty-six, still unmarried as this letter says, and regarded as a prodigy in Venice. She had spoken publicly at the University of Padua (selection 11), before the people of Venice and before the Venetian Doge (selection 7). So highly esteemed was she that she was denied permission to accept the invitation of Queen Isabella of Aragon and Sicily to join her court. It was precisely at this time that Poliziano added his veneration (for that is clearly what this letter suggests) to the fame of the learned woman.

This translation is based on the Latin text in Fedele's *Epistolae et orationes*, ed. Tomasini, pp. 155–58.[2]

## Text

OVIRGIN ORNAMENT OF ITALY,[3] how can I thank you enough for honoring me with your letter? It is nearly incredible that such a letter could have come from a woman. Did I say from a woman? On the contrary, from a girl, and a virgin. Therefore, let not previous ages any longer boast of the Muses, Sibyls,[4] or priestesses of Apollo,[5] let not the Pythagoreans boast of female philosophers,[6] let the Socratics not boast of Diotima[7] nor Aspasia,[8] and let not the records of Greece boast of those female poets, monuments of Greece:[9] Telesilla,[10] Corinna,[11] Sappho,[12] Anyte,[13] Erinna,[14] Praxilla,[15] Cleobulina,[16] and others. And now we might easily believe the Romans that the daughters of Laelius[17] and Hortensius,[18] and Cornelia, mother of the Gracchi,[19] were by far the most eloquent matrons of all. We know this, certainly, we know that [the female] sex was not by nature stupid or condemned to dullness. In the case of men, however, public praise was so free in the classical world that sometimes even slaves reached the summit of philosophy. But in our age, in which it is rare even for men to excel in letters, you are the only maiden living who handles a book instead of wool, a reed pen instead of make-up, a metal stilus instead of a needle, and who smears not her skin with white lead, but rather paper with ink. This indeed is as extraordinary, as rare, as new, as if violets took root amid ice, roses in snow or lilies in frost. But if the mere attempt is seen as a miracle, what should we say about such great progress in studies? You write a fine letter, Cassandra, sharp, elegant Latin, and although it is very sweet, with the charm of a girl and a virginal simplicity, nevertheless, it is also wise with a wonderful gravity. I have also read your oration, learned, rich, sonorous, clear and full of wide-ranging quality.[20] I have heard, too, that you are capable of extemporaneous speaking, a skill even some great orators lack. Also you are said, with the tool of dialectic, to tie knots that cannot be untangled, to disentangle knots which have never been, and will never be, untangled by others. Indeed, you have so mastered philosophy that you sharply defend and strongly attack set propositions, and you, as a virgin, dare to compete with men[21] in the beautiful race-course of learning in such a way that your sex does not daunt your soul, nor your soul your modesty, nor your modesty your talent. And although there is no one who does not exalt you with praises, nevertheless, you step forward and stem the tide of adulation as you respectfully cast down your virginal eyes. May I be allowed, O virgin, to contemplate your chaste face, so that I may marvel at your appearance, learning, and carriage, so that I may drink in as though with thirsty ears precepts, words instilled into you by your Muses, and finally, so that by your breath and inspiration, I may suddenly emerge as a complete poet. Neither Thracian Orpheus nor Linus would conquer me with songs [as you could by your words] even though Calliopea, the mother of Orpheus, be at his side, and Apollo, the father of Linus, at his.[22] Indeed, I used to marvel at Pico della Mirandola,[23] than whom no other mortal is more beautiful or more outstanding (I believe) in all branches of learning. Now behold, Cassandra, I have begun to venerate you next after Pico, perhaps now also along with him. Indeed, may the God Jupiter favor your first steps in learning, and when you depart from your parents, may a founder and consort be near who is not unworthy of your virtue, so that now that the spark of natural intellect has almost flamed by its own will, so hereafter a fuller flame, fed by breath or by kindling, may shoot forth brightly. Thus the cold night of sluggish stupidity in letters may be completely dispersed from the hearts and souls of our people.

## 24
### Girolamo Campagnola to Cassandra Fedele

## Introduction

Girolamo Campagnola (1433/1435–1522) was born in Padua. Morelli (1800) cites two Latin works of his, this letter to Cassandra Fedele, dated Venice 1514, and a panegyric on the death of Bartolomeo d'Alviano, dated Venice 1515. He is recorded as a writer and poet. It has been supposed that he was a painter, but this is not established, though he wrote on art.[1]

Cassandra Fedele was married at the age of thirty-two in 1497. Her literary studies ceased thereafter for seventeen years, resuming in 1514, as this letter suggests. Her studies were to remain sporadic for the remainder of her long life. This letter is interesting in suggesting that they ceased because of an illness contracted after her marriage. Was the illness provoked by a marriage she did not really desire and the abandonment of the studies she loved? Whatever the case, they resumed quietly with a letter on an important question of theology addressed to Fra Girolamo Monopolitano, dated May 29, 1514, the content of which is described in note 6, below. Campagnola responds to the question of theology, but also takes delight in the fact that Fedele has returned to her studies.

This translation is based on the Latin text published by C. Cavazzana, "Cassandra Fedele: erudita veneziana del Rinascimento," *L'Ateneo Veneto*, 29:2 (1906): appendix 9, 386–87.

## Text

GREETINGS, CASSANDRA, unique and outstanding light among noble women of our age.[2] Today I not only read but reread your short letter to Monopolitano, a theologian with a great name indeed.[3] The letter was most learned; and what especially delighted me was that I could perceive from this letter that you had returned to literary studies. As Cicero says, the return to literary studies is easy, because it is a return certainly to the most delightful food of souls.[4] For as you used to tell me at Padua (if I remember correctly) you had, on account of a certain illness commencing after your marriage, not only interrupted your studies of letters but indeed abandoned them. Wherefore your illness made me ill, because that radiant glory of the female sex had been utterly extinguished. Not vainly, therefore, and repeating what I said above, let me say that I am delighted that you have recovered your love of letters, for which I give thanks especially to you, your husband and your parent. With God as helper, your husband, himself a not unworthy doctor, has freed your wavering studies from sickness and restored you to the original brightness of your intellect.

As to Gregory's assertion and the question you proposed to Monopolitano,

I think that the holy man [Gregory], one of the pillars of the orthodox faith, has presented a difficulty to the human species and that few will achieve salvation. This [sad reality] has not been caused by God through his holy teacher and once high priest of the Church of God,[5] but rather by human weakness which is inclined toward sins rather than toward virtues—because of wicked pleasures and desires and innumerable enticements toward pleasures and desires.[6] As you rightly perceive, the highest God, maker of the universe, offered to the penitent and contrite his clemency and mercy as an anitdote for sins, not only to those who sin seven times but to those who sin seventy times seven,[7] like Peter in the gospel, his gatekeeper of the kingdom of heaven.[8] To us he makes it clear that man can be saved by tears alone accompanied by remorse of heart, not even requiring the rigor and severity of a hermit's life. [Of this penitence] the Magdalene is an example, as is Peter who, having denied the Savior three times, wept bitterly,[9] and the robber on the cross, who died remorseful.[10] I think, therefore, that the opinion of Gregory must be interpreted to mean that without the mercy of God the human species could not be saved. Christ himself by his own blood redeems compassionately, as you also feel—and I agree with you—and have so written in these vernacular poems long ago in which I represent the wicked soul penitent of its sins and fleeing to the divine mercy. Farewell, glory and example of noble women of our time. Venice, June 3, 1514.

*Notes*

*Bibliography*

*Index*

# Notes

Citations from the Bible are to the Revised Standard Version. The Vulgate numbering, taken from the Douay-Rheims Version, where different from the RSV, is added in parentheses and identified.

Citations from classical sources follow standard conventions for numbering. No sources are provided unless we quote from them. Most are available in the bilingual Loeb Classical Library.

For patristic and early medieval Christian writers our citations are to Jacques Paul Migne, *Patrologiae cursus completus . . . omnium SS. patrum. Series Latina*, 221 vols. + 5 supplementary vols. (Paris, 1844–56), and *Patrologiae cursus completus . . . omnium SS. patrum. Series Graeca*, 161 vols. (Paris, 1857–66). For Latin writers the designation will be PL, for Greek writers PG, followed by volume and then column number. Translations into English are cited where available. Most will be cited from two series of translations published during the latter half of the nineteenth century and often reprinted: Ante-Nicene Fathers, 10 vols., cited as ANF, followed by volume and page number; and Nicene and Post-Nicene Fathers, series 1 and 2, cited as NPNF, followed by series number, volume, and page number.

## Introduction

1. Since this anthology is intended for the general reader, bibliographical references will be kept to a minimum. The reader will be referred, however, to recent comprehensive monographs on particular figures or other sources where fuller information is available. Three recent essays provide in small compass extensive bibliographies on most of the figures dealt with here: M. L. King, "Thwarted Ambitions: Six Learned Women of the Italian Renaissance," *Soundings*, 59 (1976), biblio. app., 301–4; King, "Book-Lined Cells: Women and Humanism in the Early Italian Renaissance," in *Beyond Their Sex: Learned Women of the European Past*, ed. P. H. Labalme (New York, 1980), nn. 81–90; and P. O. Kristeller, "Learned Women of Early Modern Italy: Humanists and University Scholars," in *Beyond Their Sex*, nn. 106–16. For a comprehensive bibliography that includes women throughout Western Europe, 1350–1650, see now M. L. King, *Women of the Renaissance* (Chicago, 1991).

2. Yale University Library, MS Marston 279, fol. 2 (in gold letters): "Genevra anogarolis scripsi manu mea immaculata." We are indebted for this reference to P. O. Kristeller. See "Learned Women of Early Modern Italy," p. 112, n. 35.

3. See M. L. King, "Goddess and Captive: Antonio Loschi's Poetic Tribute to Maddalena Scrovegni (1389), Study and Text," *Medievalia et Humanistica*, n.s. 10 (1980): 103–27. The material in this section is drawn from King's study, as is the biographical material in the introduction to selection 1.

4. Bruni's letter, *De Studiis et literis*, has been translated in W. H. Woodward, *Vittorino da Feltre and Other Humanist Educators* (New York, 1963), pp. 119–33; and more recently in *The Humanism of Leonardo Bruni*, eds. G. Griffiths, J. Hankins, and D. Thompson (Binghamton, NY, 1987), pp. 240–51.

5. Woodward, pp. 123, 124.

6. Ibid., p. 126.

7. Ibid., p. 128.

8. Loc. cit.

9. Ibid., p. 129.

10. On this see N. Z. Davis, "Gender and Genre: Women as Historical Writers, 1400–1820," in *Beyond Their Sex*, chap. 8, especially pp. 153–60.

11. The writers known to us are known either through their correspondence with well-known male humanists or through citations of manuscript sources in P. O. Kristeller, *Iter Italicum*, 6 vols. (London and Leiden, 1963–92). It is not within our province to discuss humanism, about which there is a large literature. For general introductions, see E. Garin, *Italian Humanism*, trans. P. Munz (New York, 1965); P. O. Kristeller, *Renaissance Thought*, 2 vols. (New York, 1955, 1965); C. Trinkaus, *In Our Image and Likeness*, 2 vols. (Chicago, 1970); A. Rabil, Jr., ed., *Renaissance Humanism: Foundations, Forms and Legacy*, 3 vols. (Philadelphia, 1988, 2d printing in paperback, with corrections, 1991).

12. See above, n. 3.

13. Woodward, *Vittorino da Feltre*, pp. 119–20.

14. On Isotta Nogarola, see especially M. L. King, "The Religious Retreat of Isotta Nogarola (1418–66)," *Signs* 3 (1978): 807–22.

15. Quoted in King, "Thwarted Ambitions," p. 284. See A. Segarizzi, "Niccolò Barbo patrizio veneziano del secolo XV e le accuse contro Isotta Nogarola," *Giornale storico della letteratura italiana* 43 (1904): 39–54.

16. For Costanza Varano, see the bibliographical notes in King, "Book-Lined Cells," p. 83; and Kristeller, "Learned Women," p. 112.

17. For Caterina Caldiera, see M. L. King, "Personal, Domestic, and Republican Values in the Moral Philosophy of Giovanni Caldiera," *Renaissance Quarterly* 28 (1975): 537; and "Thwarted Ambitions," pp. 294–95, 303 (bibliography).

18. For Costanza Barbaro and Cecilia Gonzaga, see King, "Thwarted Ambitions," pp. 289–92, 302–3 (bibliography).

19. *De re uxoria*, ed. A. Gnesotto, *Atti e Memorie della Regia Accademia di scienze, lettere ed arti di Padova*, n. s. 32 (1915): 6–105; the preface and second book have been translated by B. G. Kohl with the title "On Wifely Duties," in *The Earthly Republic: Italian Humanists on Government and Society*, eds. Kohl and R. G. Witt (Philadelphia, 1978), pp. 179–228.

20. For Cecilia Gonzaga, see King, "Thwarted Ambitions," pp. 291–92, 302–3 (bibliography).

21. For Ippolita Sforza, see King, "Book-Lined Cells," pp. 82–83.

22. Machiavelli, *The Prince*, ed. T. G. Bergin (New York, 1947), p. 17.

23. For works to as well as by Ippolita, see indices to Kristeller, *Iter Italicum*. For the type of the woman patron, see especially W. L. Gundersheimer, "Women, Learning, and Power: Eleonora of Aragon and the Court of Ferrara," in *Beyond Their Sex*, pp. 43–65.

24. For Cassandra Fedele, see King, "Thwarted Ambitions," pp. 295–99, 304 (bibliography).

25. For Laura Cereta, see A. Rabil, Jr., *Laura Cereta: Quattrocento Humanist* (Binghamton, 1981), part 1.

26. For Alessandra Scala, see King, "Learned Women," p. 113.

27. See below, selection 17, n. 4.

28. The most notable exception is Christine de Pizan (1363?–1431), a younger contemporary of most of the women humanists of Italy, whose accomplishments as an historical writer far outstripped their work. The standard biography is now C. C. Willard, *Christine de Pizan: Her Life and Works* (New York, 1984). See also E. J. Richards, "Introduction," *The Book of the City of Ladies* by Christine de Pizan (New York, 1982), xix–xlvi; Davis, "Gender and Genre: Women as Historical Writers, 1400–1820," pp. 157–60; and M. L. King, *Women of the Renaissance* (Chicago, 1991).

29. The most striking exception to this statement is the career of Ermolao Barbaro, whose defense of celibacy was based on his desire to free himself from the political obligations of the Venetian government, in order to be able to pursue the study of philosophy. See M. L. King, "Caldiera and the Barbaros on Marriage and Family: Humanist Reflections of Venetian Realities," *The Journal of Medieval and Renaissance Studies* 6 (1976): 35–44.

30. Castiglione, *The Courtier*, book 3, par. 9ff. There are two recent unabridged English translations, one by C. S. Singleton (Garden City, NY, 1959), the other by G. Bull (New York, 1967).

31. Important examples of these court ladies were Elizabetta Gonzaga, Isabella d'Este, and Battista Sforza, mentioned above, p. 23. See also above, n. 23. Isabella d'Este did write a number of letters on many subjects, though in Italian rather than in Latin.

32. For some of these women, see R. H. Bainton, *Women of the Reformation in Germany and Italy* (Minneapolis, 1971), part 2. See especially chap. 15 on Olympia Morata.

33. *The Colloquies of Erasmus*, trans. C. R. Thompson (Chicago, 1965), pp. 217–23. Erasmus also expresses his views about the education of women (thinking of Sir Thomas More's children in particular) in his *Opus epistolarum*, ed. P. S. Allen *et al.* (Oxford, 1906–58), Ep. 1233, 4, 578: 103–579:149; *The Correspondence of Erasmus*, trans. R.A.B. Mynors and D.F.S. Thomson, Collected Works of Erasums (Toronto, 1974–), 8:297–98 (lines 112–62).

34. *The Colloquies of Erasmus*, p. 219.

## Selection 1

1. Other letters are known to be extant in manuscript: Milan, Biblioteca Am-

brosiana, cod. C141 inf., fols. 150r–168r; cf. Kristeller, *Iter Italicum*, 1:319–20.

2. Psalm 98:1 (97:1, Vulgate).

3. Psalm 98:2 (97:2, Vulgate).

4. Psalm 40:1–2 (39:2–3, Vulgate).

5. Psalm 40:3 (39:4, Vulgate).

6. Psalm 81: 1 (80:2, Vulgate). — The Prince mentioned a few sentences later is Giangaleazzo Visconti (1351–1402), who seized power in Milan in 1385 and was named Duke in 1395 by the Emperor Wenceslaus.

7. Psalm 9:14–15 (9:16, Vulgate).

8. Revelation 14:13.

9. Revelation 19:1–2. The tyrant here is Francesco il Vecchio da Carrara (1325–1388, ruler 1350–1388), recently deposed.

10. Psalm 52:5–7 (51:7–9, Vulgate).

11. Psalm 28:4 (27:4, Vulgate).

12. Isaiah 28:17.

13. Isaiah 29:7.

## Selection 2

1. Vitelleschi had been appointed a bishop in 1431. Later, for these and other exploits (notably restoring order in Rome after a rebellion in 1434) he was appointed patriarch of Alexandria (1435), archbishop of Florence (1435), and cardinal (1437). He was finally seized in Rome in 1440 and imprisoned in the Castel Sant' Angelo where the pope allowed his life to be taken.

2. Cf. Hebrews 12:35–38.

3. Demosthenes (384–322 B.C.E.) was the most famous of Greek orators.

## Selection 3

1. For other versions of the Latin text, see the editions cited in King, "Book-Lined Cells," p. 83.

2. Cicero (106–43 B.C.E.) was the greatest orator produced by Republican Rome and the model for humanists in Renaissance Italy.

3. Latium originally referred to the area of central Italy around Rome but soon gained the extended sense of the Roman homeland, Italy, as it is used here.

4. Cicero *Pro Marcello* 2. 5.

## Selection 4

1. For other versions of the Latin text, see the editions cited in "Book-Lined Cells," p. 83.

2. See above, selection 2, n. 1.

3. In 1204, Venice urged crusading forces transported on her ships to sack

Constantinople, ostensibly to drive out schismatic Greeks ruled by the pseudo-emperor Alexius IV, and restore legitimate rule. Actually the motivation for this event was sheer greed and its effect was to weaken the Christian Byzantine Empire. It is probably this well-known event that Costanza had in mind.

4. Aristotle *Nicomachean Ethics* 8. 10–11 (1160a–1161b). This treatise had been translated from Greek into Latin earlier in the century by both Giannozzo Manetti and Leonardo Bruni.

5. Cicero *Pro Marcello* 4. 11.

## Selection 5

1. Aetna is Europe's highest active volcano (over 10,000 feet). It is in Sicily. Virgil mentions it in the *Aeneid* 3. 570–81.

2. Cf. Cicero *De officiis* 1. 7. 22.

3. See Cicero *Tusculan Disputations* 1. 15. 34. Cicero is quoting the older poet Ennius and contending that the writer seeks fame and immortality through his work. So will Ippolita, by imitating her mother, achieve the same.

## Selection 6

1. *Memoirs of a Renaissance Pope: The Commentaries of Pius II*, trans. F. A. Gragg, ed. L. C. Gabel (New York, 1962), p. 116.

2. Ibid., p. 117.

3. For other editions, see Corvisieri, xii.

## Selection 7

1. It was common in antiquity to mark a "happy day" with a pebble. See Catullus, 68. 148 and 106. 6.

2. See Virgil *Eclogues* 1. 59.

3. Thamyris, Queen of Scythia, destroyed the army of Cyrus in a battle in which Cyrus himself was killed. Hypsicratea followed her husband Mithridates into war and became as strong and resilient as any soldier. On both see Giovanni Boccaccio, *De claris mulieribus*, ed. V. Zaccaria, in *Tutte le opere di Giovanni Boccaccio*, ed. V. Branca (Milan, 1967; 2d ed. 1970), vol. 10, Latin and Italian on facing pages; *Concerning Famous Women*, trans. G. A. Guarino (New Brunswick, N.J., 1963), chaps. 47 and 76.

## Selection 8

1. Both were granddaughters of Battista da Montefeltro Malatesta.

2. Eubel lists a Pandulfus d'Almiano as apostolic protonotary of Camerino, May

30, 1431 until his death on March 4, 1437. He has a listing for Patras (in Greece) but the earliest listing is for 1473. Gams also lists Pandulfus but has no listing at all for Patras. See C. Eubel, *Hierarchia Catholica Medii Aevi* (Regensburgiana, 1914; reprinted, Padua, 1960), vol. 2 (1431–1503), pp. 116, 213; and P. B. Gams, *Series Episcoporum Ecclesiae Catholicae* (Graz, 1957), p. 679.

    3. Virgil *Aeneid* 1. 374. The translation is that of F. O. Copley, *Virgil: The Aeneid* (Indianapolis, 1965), p. 13.

## Selection 9

    1. The poem is found in Nogarola, *Opera*, ed. Abel, 2:7, line 7.

    2. Lactantius, *Divinae Institutiones*, 2.2 (PL 6:260); *Divine Institutes*, ANF, 7:41–42.

    3. Cicero *De officiis* 1. 6. 18.

    4. Quintilian, 1. 1. 1.

    5. Aspasia lived with Pericles as his mistress from about 450 until his death in 429. Her intellectual attainments were great, as attested by the Socratics, e.g., Aeschines. A son she bore Pericles was legitimated after the death of the two sons he had by his wife (whom he divorced to live with Aspasia). See Plutarch *Life of Pericles* 24. 1–7.

    6. Cornelia was the daughter of Scipio Africanus. Her home was a model of Greek culture, and after the death of her husband Tiberius Gracchus in 154 B.C.E. she refused to marry again but concentrated on educating her three surviving children: Tiberius, Gaius, and Sempronia. Although Plutarch in his lives, *Tiberius and Caius Gracchus*, 1.1–5, discusses Cornelia, Varano's source was probably Valerius Maximus 6.1; Pliny, *Natural History*, 7.36; or Cicero, *On Divination*, 1.18.36; 2.29.62.

    7. Elphe is perhaps Elpinice, the sister of Cimon who so pleaded with Pericles on her brother's behalf when he was on trial for his life—after having failed to take Macedon as he could have done—that Pericles, one of Cimon's accusers, hardly spoke against him in court, with the result that Cimon was acquitted. She is mentioned in this connection in Plutarch's *Life of Pericles* 10. 4–5 and his *Life of Cimon* 14. 2–4.

## Selection 10

    1. Augustine, *De Genesi ad litteram*, 12.11.35 (PL 34:449); *The Literal Meaning of Genesis*, trans. J. M. Taylor, Ancient Christian Writers, vols. 41–42 (New York, 1982), 42: 68–69.

    2. The original letters are extant in at least three manuscript versions: Florence, Biblioteca Nazionale Centrale, cod. xxxviii, 142, fols. 117–33; Naples, Biblioteca Nazionale, cod. V. B. 35, fols. 27–42; Rome, Biblioteca dell'Accademia Nazionale dei Lincei e Corsiniana, cod. 839 (43 D 8), fols. 67v–75.

    3. For Ludovico Foscarini, see the bibliog. n. 27 in King, "The Religious Retreat of Isotta Nogarola," p. 813.

4. Peter Lombard, *Sententiae in IV Libris Distinctae*, book 2, distinction 21, chap. 5, par. 2 (PL 192:696).

5. Genesis 3:4, 5.

6. Genesis 2:15–17.

7. Genesis 3:6.

8. The closest parallel in thought to this statement is I Corinthians 15:22: "For as in Adam all die, so in Christ all will be made to live."

9. Genesis 3:16.

10. Genesis 3:17–19.

11. I Corinthians 14:38.

12. Aristotle *Nicomachean Ethics* 3. 5. 1113b. 30–33.

13. Cf. I Corinthians 1:27–29; 8:1.

14. Ecclesiasticus 10:13.

15. Orosius was a friend of Augustine's who wrote, at Augustine's request, *Historiarum libri septem* (PL 31: 635–1212); *Seven Books of History Against the Pagans*, trans. I. W. Raymond (New York, 1936). Orosius addressed several questions to Augustine about the errors of the Priscillians and Origenists (PL 31:1211–16), drawing from Augustine a reply, the only work Augustine addressed to Orosius: *Ad Orosium contra Priscillianistas et Origenistas liber unus* (PL 42:669–78; for the reference in our text, see 671). Nogarola may also have been reading Augustine's *On Free Will*, 3:25.76, where Augustine cites Ecclesiasticus 10:12–13 (which she has just cited) and then adds a passage very similar to hers: "To the devil's pride was added malevolent envy, so that he persuaded man to show the same pride as had proved the devil's damnation." (PL 32:1308); *Augustine: Earlier Writings*, Library of Christian Classics 6, trans. J. H. S. Burleigh (Philadelphia, 1953), p. 216.

16. Genesis 3:5.

17. The general notion that Eve's pride caused her to sin is in *De Genesi ad litteram*, 11.30 (PL 34: 445); *The Literal Meaning of Genesis*, 42:162.

18. The idea that the sin of Adam was fortunate because it made necessary Christ the redeemer appears throughout the history of Christian theology.

19. See Aristotle *Posterior Analytics* 2. 11–12. 94a20–96a19.

20. *Posterior Analytics* 2. 13. 96a24–96b24.

21. This general idea is expressed through the passage in the preceding note.

22. St. Gregory, *Liber regulae pastoralis*, 3.32 (PL 77:115); *St. Gregory's Pastoral Rule*, NPNF, ser. 2, 12:65.

23. Ibid., 1.2 (PL 77:15–16; NPNF, ser. 2, 12:2).

24. In the more historical synoptic Gospels, there is only one exchange between Jesus and Pilate. Pilate asks Jesus whether he is the king of the Jews, to which Jesus responds: "You have said so." In the Gospel of John there are three exchanges between the two, but none of them approaches the quotation in this text. Neither is there anything resembling this statement in the apocryphal *Acts of Pilate* or other apocryphal literature related to the New Testament in which Pilate is mentioned.

25. Genesis 1:26.

26. Genesis 2:18.

27. Ambrose, *Expositio in Lucam*, 9:23 (PL 15:1891).

28. "All men by nature desire to know" is the first sentence in Aristotle's *Metaphysics*.

29. Matthew 19:17.

30. Mark 10:17ff.; Matthew 19:16–17; Luke 18:18ff.

31. The idea appears throughout *On Nature and Grace*. A passage very close to this one is in chap. 67 (PL 44:286–88; NPNF, ser. 1, 5:145).

32. Ambrose, *De Paradiso*, 8.39 (PL 14:309); *Hexameron, Paradise, and Cain and Abel*, trans. J. J. Savage, Fathers of the Church 42 (New York, 1961), pp. 316–18.

33. Genesis 2:23.

34. Gregory, *Moralium libri*, 4.36.62 (PL 75:670–71); *Morals on the Book of Job*, 3 vols., trans. J. Bliss (Oxford, 1844–50).

35. There is no book on the Trinity by Isidore, and he does not say precisely what is said here in his discussion of the Trinity or the sacraments in his *Etymologiae*, 7.1–4 (PL 82:259–72).

36. *De Genesi ad litteram*, 8.17–19 (PL 34:387); *The Literal Meaning of Genesis*, 42:58–60.

37. Psalm 69:4 (68:5, Vulgate).

38. Romans 5:12: "Therefore as through one man sin entered into the world and through sin death, and thus death has passed unto all men because all have sinned—"

39. We do not find this precise statement, but we do find two statements very close to it in *On Grace and Free Choice*, 1.2 and 4.9 (PL 182:1002, 1006–7); *The Works of Bernard of Clairvaux, Volume 7, On Grace and Free Choice*, trans. D. O'Donovan, intro. B. McGinn (Kalamazoo, MI, 1977), pp. 55–56, 65.

40. Augustine, *De Genesi ad litteram*, 11.9–16 (PL 34:434–58); *The Literal Meaning of Genesis*, 42:141–48.

41. The idea that the mind has direct contact with God apart from the sense world is the most characteristic of Augustinian ideas and one of the principal notions that sets "Augustinianism" apart from "Thomism." The idea expressed here may be found throughout the *Confessions* and *On True Religion*, among other works.

42. Ecclesiasticus 15:14–15 (15:14–16, Vulgate): "It was he who created man in the beginning, and he left him in the power of his own inclination. If you will, you can keep the commandments, and to act faithfully is a matter of your own choice."

43. Genesis 3:12.

44. John 15:22.

45. John 11:47.

46. Mark 14:61; Matthew 26:63; Luke 22:67, 70.

47. Matthew 15:24, 26.

48. Boethius, *De consolatione philosophae*, 3. prose 5 (PL 63:743); *The Consolation of Philosophy*, trans. R. Green (New York, 1962), p. 52.

49. Cf. Catiline's famous remark *incendium meum ruina restinguam* as reported in Sallust, *Catiline*, 31. 9 and in Cicero *Pro Murena* 25. 51.

## Selection 11

1. See Kristeller, "Learned Women of Early Modern Italy," *Beyond Their Sex*, 98ff.

2. According to Professor Benjamin Kohl he is mentioned in A. Riccoboni, *De gymnasio patavino* (Padua, 1985), p. 18; and in A. Zambaldi, *Monumenti storici di Concordia* (San Vito, 1840), p. 112. We have seen neither of these texts.

2a. There are also earlier printed versions, the earliest, perhaps, that of Venice, 1488; cf. H. Simonsfeld, "Zur Geschichte der Cassandra Fedele," in *Studien zur Literaturgeschichte, Michael Bernays Gewidmet von Schülern und Freunden* (Hamburg and Leipzig, 1893), pp. 101ff.

3. See Cicero, *Tusculan Disputations*, 5.30.84–85.

4. This could be a reference to the Greek city in Boeotia, once the chief Mycenean city in central Greece. But the reference may also be to Thebes, the capital of Egypt, famed for its temples.

5. See Horace, *Odes*, 1.38.1. Cyrus (559–529 B.C.E.) was the founder of the Persian Empire, taking Lydia, Babylonia, Assyria, Syria, and Palestine. He respected the customs and religion of the peoples he conquered. To the Greeks he was the model of an upright ruler.

6. Darius (521–486 B.C.E.) was King of Persia. He suppressed the Ionian Greek cities in 499. To punish the Greeks who came to the aid of the Ionians he invaded Greece in 490 but was defeated at Marathon.

7. Philip was King of Macedon, 359–336 B.C.E., founder of the Macedonian Empire and father of Alexander the Great (356–323 B.C.E.), who studied with Aristotle, took the reins of empire upon his father's death and extended his conquests throughout the Near Eastern World.

8. Lycurgus is the traditional founder of the Spartan constitution. His dates are uncertain, though Spartan life was not developed to the point he is said to have brought it before the sixth century. There is, in fact, some doubt whether he is an historical figure at all or only one of the gods worshipped in the Peloponnesus to whom almost everything peculiarly Spartan was later attributed. See Herodotus, 1.66; and Plutarch, *Life of Lycurgus*. Fedele would not have needed to know these Greek sources. Lycurgus was often mentioned by Latin writers. See, e.g., Cicero, *Tusculan Disputations*, 1.110; 5.7–8; Valerius Maximus, 2.6.1; 5.3.Ext.2.

9. Hercules was the son of Jove and Alcmena, noted for his great strength. The story of many of his exploits is recounted in Ovid, *Metamorphoses*, 9.1–330.

10. Spurinna was a beautiful young Etruscan boy who, in order not to arouse desire among women, disfigured his face. See Valerius Maximus 3.5.Ext.1.

11. Croesus (560–546 B.C.E.) was the last king of Lydia, conquered by the Persians under Cyrus. He is discussed at length in Herodotus, 1.25–95. Fedele's source was probably Valerius Maximus 5.4.Ext.6.

12. The reference is to Tomyris or Thamyris, queen of the Massagetae, whose army defeated the Persians in a battle in which Cyrus was killed. The story of her role and her behavior after his death is told in Herodotus, 1.213–15. Fedele's source was probably Boccaccio, *Concerning Famous Women*, ch. 47; or Valerius Maximus, 9.10.Ext.1.

13. Xerxes was the son of Darius (see above, n. 6), King of Persia, 485–465 B.C.E. The reference here is to his famous invasion of Greece in 480 which ended in his defeat in the battle of Salamis and his retreat to Persia. The invasion, a major threat to Greek civilization, is the main theme in Herodotus' history (bks. 5–9). The event was widely known, however, from many sources.

14. Stratonicus (ca. 410–360 B.C.E.) was an Athenian musician and wit, many of whose sayings were collected soon after his death. Atheneus collected many of them in *The Learned Banquet*, 8.347–52, though the one cited here is not among them. We have been unable to locate the source in which she might have found it.

15. Plato, *Republic*, 5.471C–474B.

16. The passage which follows down through the mention of Zoroaster in the next sentence, with the exception of the mention of the priests of Cybele, is taken from Diogenes Laertius, 1.prologue, 1–5. Cybele was the great mother-goddess of Anatolia, primarily a goddess of fertility. Her chief sanctuary was in Phrygia, but the cult appears at an early date in Lydia and by the fifth century in Greece. It was brought to Rome from Asia Minor in 205–204 B.C.E., the first mystery religion of the Near East to be established in Rome. What its connection is with the founding of philosophy is not clear. The authority for all the other assertions here, however, clearly derives from Diogenes Laertius.

17. Johannes Regius was Giovanni Regio from Venice who, for a time around 1500, served as librarian at the Vatican under Pope Alexander VI. He was author of a commentary on Plutarch, now lost. See C. Jöchers, *Allgemeines Gelehrten Lexikon* (Leipzig, 1751), 3:1963–64.

## Selection 12

1. Giorgio Valla (1447–1499) was born in Piacenza and died in Venice. Among his teachers were George of Trebizond and Constantine Lascaris. He taught at Pavia between 1466 and 1476, then at Milan and Genoa, before settling in Venice in 1485, where he taught in the public school of rhetoric for many years. Giovanni Pierio Valeriano, a son of Ludovico il Moro, as well as the sons of many Venetian noblemen, were among his pupils. He was also centrally involved in the printing of books which was flourishing in Venice and owned a splendid library of printed books and manuscripts. He wrote on many subjects. See J. L. Heiberg, "Beiträge zur Geschichte Georg Vallas und seiner Bibliothek," *Centralblatt für Bibliothekswesen*, Beiheft 13 (1896): 353–482.

2. Patched together here from two different contexts are two passages from Lucan's *Pharsalia*. The first passage is a speech by Caesar and the second a reference to the sad fate of Pompey. The only thing they have in common is that they both mention *Fortuna*. The translation is that of J. D. Duff, *Lucan*, (Cambridge, MA, 1977), 387–89, 489.

3. Plato *Republic* 5. 471C–474B.

4. Plato *Republic* 6. 494.

5. On Philip and Alexander, see above, selection 11, n. 7. The point is that

Philip was glad Aristotle could educate Alexander. See Aulus Gellius *Noctes Atticae* 9. 3. 1ff.

## Selection 13

1. Presumably he was disturbed because she was living among rustic people (she refers to this negatively in another letter) and had removed herself from the learned urban environment.

2. The allusion is to holy women of biblical times. Sarah was the half-sister and wife of Abraham, mother of Isaac (Genesis 11ff.). Esther was a Jewish heroine who saved her people from destruction (Esther). Susanna gave her means to aid Jesus (Luke 8:3). But the intended reference here is probably the heroine of *The History of Susanna*, added to the book of Daniel; Susanna refused the sexual advances of two Jewish elders who then accused her of adultery with an imaginary youth; she was condemned to death, but Daniel convicted the elders of false testimony and they were executed. Sephora (Zipporah) was Moses' wife (Exodus 4:24–26). Sapphira appears in Acts 5:1ff., but her behavior is anything but exemplary or heroic and does not fit this context.

3. Cleopatra was Antony's mistress before and after his marriage to Octavian's sister. The image of the two here is probably drawn from Boccaccio, *Concerning Famous Women*, chap. 86. Rebecca was the daughter of Abraham's brother who was brought from the land of Aram to marry Isaac, lest he marry a Canaanite (see Genesis 24).

4. Paris abducted Helen, the wife of Menelaus, bringing on the Trojan War. She is treated in Homer and the tragedians, among others in Greek literature. She is also mentioned by the Roman poets, who generally take a critical (moralistic) view of her. Rachel was the daughter of Laban. Jacob the Patriarch worked for Laban for fourteen years in order to marry her. She was the mother of Joseph and Benjamin (in giving birth to whom she died), the best-loved of Jacob's twelve children (see Genesis 29ff.).

5. A contrast could be intended here between the few who attend church and the many who attend weddings. But it is more likely that the intention is to suggest the preoccupation with fine apparel, whether attending church or weddings.

6. Cf. Juvenal *Satires*, 6. 502ff.

7. Cf. Juvenal *Satires*, 6. 461ff.

8. Literally the last phrase reads: "to avenge our sins an army of Turks rises up against the Cenomani?" The Cenomani were Gauls who generally supported Rome. But in 200 B.C.E. they joined Hamilcar and were subjugated and Romanized, disappearing from history (Livy, 31.10; 32.30).

9. Cf. Quintilian, 8. preface, par. 26: "But nowadays our rhetoricians regard Cicero as lacking both polish and learning; we are far superior, for we look upon everything that is dictated by nature as beneath our notice, and seek not for the true ornaments of speech, but for meretricious finery (*qui non ornamenta quaerimus sed lenocinia*). . . . Cereta's phrase reads: *Ornamenta, non lenocinia sequamur*. . . . The

contrast here between "honors" and "allurements" is between "ornamentation" and "lavish dress" or "dressing like whores."

10. The first four names recall famous Romans. The last, of course, is the name of this correspondent, who is being identified with past men of fame. The Brutus intended here is doubtless Lucius Junius Brutus, consul in 509, who expelled the Tarquins and became the traditional founder of the Roman republic (see Livy, 1.56; 2.3–6; Juvenal, 8.265–70). Manius Curius Dentatus (consul 209, 284, 275, 274) and Gaius Fabricius Luscinus (consul 282, 278) were both conquerors of Pyrrhus, among others, and were celebrated by Cicero as typical examples of Roman virtue (see Cicero, *Paradoxa*, 50). Fabius (275–203 B.C.E.) was a famous Roman general who, during the Second Punic War, used delaying tactics against Hannibal, refusing to fight the Carthaginians in open battle. The merits of his policy were later acknowledged (see Livy, 22–30, passim). There were several famous Catos. Probably the one intended is Marcus Porcius Cato (234–149 B.C.E.), Cato the Censor, whose name is a byword for austerity and Puritanism. He wanted to return to the simpler Roman life and virtues. There were also several famous Aemiliuses. The first was Marcus Aemilius Lepidus (d. 152 B.C.E.), associated with the pacification of Gaul (see Livy, 41.19). Two others of the same name lived in the first century B.C.E.

11. This last paragraph is surely a reference to Isotta Nogarola's Dialogue on Adam and Eve (selection 10). Cereta appears to be backing down from her defense of women, but she is doing so satirically, turning the tables on Aemilius, so to speak, and putting him on the defensive.

## Selection 14

1. Literally the text reads: "blind Medusa by dropping oil [into her eyes]."

2. Phoebus Apollo, i.e., the Sun.

3. We find no reference to an Ethiopian Sabba. But in the Hebrew Bible Saba is Sheba and in this case would mean the Queen of Sheba, who visited the court of the Hebrew King, Solomon, posing to him certain riddles to test his proverbial wisdom (see I Kings 10; II Chronicles 9 [III Kings 10; II Paralipomenon 9, in Vulgate]).

4. See Boccaccio, *Concerning Famous Women*, chap. 24.

5. See ibid., chap. 19.

6. Ibid., chap. 25.

7. Ibid., chap. 8.

8. On her and the qualities mentioned, see ibid., chap. 98.

9. Ibid., chap. 28.

10. Apollo was the god of higher aspects of civilization, among them philosophy. He was said, for example, to be the father of Plato. The reference to secret writings suggests nothing specific, perhaps a tradition associated with the Oracle at Delphi, Apollo's principal sanctuary.

11. Diogenes Laertius twice mentions Lastheneia as a disciple of Plato. Lastheneia of Mantinea is mentioned both times together with Axiothea of Phlius. One reference states that they wore men's clothes, the other that they attended Plato's

lectures and that Plato was derided for having an "Arcadian girl" as his pupil (3. 46; 4. 2). We find no reference to Philiasia or to the tradition that they tricked the disciples of Plato with clever sophistries.

12. Sappho (b. 612 B.C.E) of Lesbos is among the most famous of Greek poets and poetesses. Her poems were collected into seven books. A number of fragments are extant. Her poems have been rendered into English a number of times. See S. Q. Groden, *The Poems of Sappho* (Indianapolis, IN, 1966). Cereta's source was doubtless Boccaccio, *Concerning Famous Women*, chap. 45.

13. Boccaccio, *Concerning Famous Women*, chap. 58.

14. Ibid., chap. 95.

15. Ibid., chap. 2, discusses Semiramis, a Queen of the Assyrians. We find no reference to a Greek Semiamira.

16. Ibid., chap. 74.

17. Ibid., chap. 82.

18. Ibid., chap. 84.

19. Tulliola or Tullia was born in 78 B.C.E. and died in 45 B.C.E. Cicero loved her dearly and considered building a temple to her after her death, which was a turning point in his mental life. See R. E. Proctor, *Education's Great Amnesia: Reconsidering the Humanities from Petrarch to Freud* (Bloomington, IN, 1988), pp. 59–63.

20. Terentia, perhaps Cicero's wife and the mother of Tullia (above). She exercised a great influence on her husband on numerous occasions, including that of the Catiline conspiracy. The two were divorced in 46 B.C.E after Cicero returned from exile. She is reputed to have lived to the age of 103. See *The Oxford Classical Dictionary*, p. 885.

21. See above, selection 9, n. 6.

22. Isotta Nogarola and Cassandra Fedele are well represented in this anthology. See the editors' introduction for biographical details about them. About Nicolosa Sanuto of Bologna little is known. An oration said to be by her, arguing that women be permitted to dress luxuriously, is extant but credited by contemporaries to Filelfo. See P. O. Kristeller, "Learned Women of Early Modern Italy," pp. 96 and 110–11, n. 30.

## *Selection 15*

1. A reference to the Roman practice of placing votes in an urn (after legislation between 139 and 107 B.C.E. to guarantee the secrecy of voting), which were then counted to determine the will of the majority of the tribes voting.

2. Megaera was one of the Furies. Virgil places them in the underworld where they punish evildoers. The Greek poets thought of them as pursuing sinners on earth. They were inexorable but just. The allusion is thus not entirely accurate, since Cereta intends to say that although these women are Furies in their pursuit of others, the pursuit itself is unjust.

## Selection 16

1. On Alessandra Scala, see G. Pesenti, "Alessandra Scala, una figurina della Rinascenza fiorentina," *Giornale storico della letteratura italiana*, 85 (1925): 241–67.

2. We do not find this precise statement, but in the *Republic* 5. 475–76 we find the idea that one who has a passion for wisdom has not only curiosity but also the desire to behold reality (form) itself.

## Selection 17

1. See P. Preto in *DBI* 29 (1983): 497–500; and M. L. King, *Venetian Humanism in an Age of Patrician Dominance* (Princeton, 1986), pp. 355–57.

2. The passage is quoted in W. H. Woodward, *Vittorino da Feltre*, p. 66.

3. See *Epistolae*, ed. Mehus (1759), 2: 418–19.

4. Woodward, *Vittorino da Feltre*, p. 76.

5. The text was previously published in Edmond Martène and Ursin Durand, eds., *Veterum scriptorum et monumentorum historicorum, dogmaticorum, moralium, amplissima collectio*, vol. 3 (Paris, 1724), cols. 829–42.

6. *Epistola ad novitium Carthusianum de commodis vitae regularis*, in Contarini, *Anecdota Veneta*, pp. 24–32.

7. Psalm 127:1 (126:1, Vulgate).

8. The letters of Jerome referred to are doubtless the letter to Eustochium # 22 (PL 22:384–425; NPNF, ser. 2, 6:22–41) written in 384, in which Jerome lays down the motives which ought to actuate those who remain virgins, and the rules for regulating their daily conduct; and a similar letter to Demetrias # 130 (PL 22:1107–24; NPNF, ser. 2, 6:260–72), written thirty years later in 414. Migne contains no letter from Ambrose to Demetrias.

9. See especially Augustine's treatises *De continentia*, *De bono conjugali* (where virginity is explicitly preferred), and *De sancta virginitate* (PL 40:345–428); *On Continence*, *On the Good of Marriage*, and *On Virginity* (NPNF, ser. 1, 3:377–438).

10. The reference is to the Florentine Ambrogio Traversari (1386–1439), a member and later General of the Camaldulensian Order, among the first generation of humanists to learn Greek thoroughly and to translate many works from Greek into Latin. The treatise referred to here is doubtless *De vera integritate virginitatis*, in which virgin chastity is glorified. Although during the Renaissance this treatise was attributed to St. Basil of Caesarea, modern scholars now believe it was written by Basil of Ancyra (d. c. 364). See C. L. Stinger, *Humanism and the Church Fathers* (Albany, 1977), pp. 126–27.

11. See especially Jerome, *Contra Jovinianum* (PL 23:221–352); *Against Jovinian* (NPNF, ser. 2, 6:346–416).

12. Revelation 14:4.

13. Matthew 19:11.

14. Matthew 19:12.

15. I Corinthians 7:26. Our Latin text reads: "I wish all men to be as I am," but the RSV reads (and the modern Vulgate rendering agrees with it): "it is well for a person to remain as he is."

16. I Corinthians 7:34.

17. Psalm 54:6 (Vulgate, 53:8).

18. I Corinthians 7:28.

19. Genesis 3:16.

20. Virgil *Eclogues* 4. 6. The translation is that of C. D. Lewis, *The Eclogues and Georgics of Virgil* (Garden City, N. Y., 1964), p. 35.

21. Matthew 10:37.

22. Psalm 45:10 (44:11, Vulgate).

23. Psalm 45:13–15 (44:14–16, Vulgate).

24. Mark 1:6; Matthew 3:4.

25. Job 7:1.

26. Romans 7:23.

27. See II Corinthians 6:4ff.; 11:27–29; 12:10.

28. Chiron is one of the Centaurs, a wise and kind old man of divine origin, well-versed in medicine (*Iliad* 4. 219) and other arts. Melampus was a prophet, missionary of Dionysus, ancestor of the prophetic clan of the Melampodidae (see *Odyssey* 11. 290). The story of the Good Samaritan is told in Luke 10:29–37.

29. Colossians 3:5 (in part).

30. Romans 14:21.

31. See Jerome, Ep. 14.4 (PL 22:349; NPNF, ser. 2, 3:15).

32. See Daniel 1:8–16; I Kings 17 (III Kings 17, Vulgate).

33. Job 1:4–5.

34. Ecclesiastes 7:3.

35. Apicius was a gourmet who lived during the reigns of the Roman emperors Augustus and Tiberius. Both Seneca and Juvenal mention the fact that he committed his experience in cuisine to writing, but the work *De re coquinaria*, compiled under his name, actually was written several centuries later.

36. Virgil *Aeneid* 3. 483.

37. Galatians 5:17.

38. I John 2:16.

39. See Virgil *Eclogues* 6. 71.

40. Proverbs 21:1.

41. See Genesis 19:1–28.

42. St. Cecilia (second or third century) was one of the most venerated martyrs in the early Roman church. According to her acts which are apocryphal and date from the end of the fifth century, she converted her pagan husband, Valerian, and his brother, Tibertius, and both were martyred for the faith before her. See *The Oxford Dictionary of the Christian Church*, pp. 253–54.

43. We cannot identify this allusion.

44. I Timothy 5:13.

45. See Romans 2:6–11.

46. Psalm 118:15–16, (117:16, Vulgate).

47. See Matthew 14:28–31.

48. These are all fathers of the Latin church: Lactantius (c. 240–c. 320), called "The Christian Cicero;" Cyprian (d.258), Bishop of Carthage; Hilary (c. 316–67), defender of the Athanasian view of God in the west and proclaimed one of the Doctors of the Church by Pius IX in 1851; Jerome (c. 342–420), Christian scholar par excellence, already encountered several times in this letter; Ambrose (c. 339–

97), Bishop of Milan, famous as a preacher; Augustine (354–430), greatest of Latin patristic theologians, most widely read theologian in the western church; Gregory (c. 540–604), pope from 590, called Gregory the Great and, along with Ambrose, Jerome and Augustine, one of the traditional four doctors of the Latin church; Leo the Great (d. 461), pope from 440, important in the development of the Chalcedonian Creed on the two natures of Christ in 451; Cassian (c. 360–435), a monk who transferred eastern monasticism to the west, writing two treatises (*Conferences* and *Institutes*) which stand behind the development of western monasticism; Sulpitius (c. 363–c. 420/5), author of a history of the church from creation to 400 A.D.; Bernard (1090–1153), real founder of the Cistercian Order, the most powerful and influential monk of his time, the epitome of the monk in an age in which that profession was the most highly venerated; Salvianus was a leading ascetic after 430 (d. c. 450), author of numerous works on asceticism, mostly lost.

49. Gregory of Nyssa (c. 330–c. 395) was one of the Cappadocian Fathers instrumental in the development of the final doctrine of the Trinity at Constantinople in 381; Basil (330–379) was also one of the Cappadocian Fathers, as well as author of a monastic rule important in the east; Chrysostom (c. 347–407), Bishop of Constantinople, was named "golden mouth" for his eloquence as a preacher; Athanasius (c. 296-373), was Bishop of Alexandria, the most important theologian and politician in combatting Arianism and setting the stage for Constantinople and the orthodox doctrine of the Trinity; John Climacus (c. 570–649) was an ascetic and writer on the spiritual life; and Ephraem Syrus (c. 306–373) was a Syrian biblical exegete.

50. Originally an unidentified thirteenth-century French work from which several Latin translations, one Italian translation, and an English translation were made in the later fourteenth and fifteenth centuries. The work "presents with fervent feeling the progress of a typical soul from the earlier ranges of spiritual life to its highest reaches. The form is largely dialogue, the participants being Love, Virtue, Reason, Holy Church, *et al.*" J. E. Wells, *A Manual of the Writings in Middle English, 1050–1400* (New Haven, 1932), Fifth Supplement, 1362, item 464.

51. See Jerome, letter 22, PL 22:409; NPNF, ser. 2, 6:31.

52. Hilary is traditionally regarded as the earliest Latin hymn writer. The five hymns attributed to him, however, are no longer believed to have been composed by him. The one referred to here is *Lucis largitor splendide*, a morning hymn. A spurious letter to his imaginary daughter, Abra, was apparently written for the purpose of attributing this hymn to Hilary. The hymns, together with other works attributed to Hilary, have been published in J. F. Gamurrini, *S. Hilarii Tractatus de Mysteriis et Humni* (Rome, 1887), 4 vols. For a discussion of the problem, see NPNF, ser. 2, 9:xlvi–xlviii.

53. Virgil *Aeneid* 6. 56: *Phoebe gravis Troiae semper miserate labores*, "Phoebus, help ever-present in Troy's dark days." The translation is that of F. O. Copley, *Virgil: The Aeneid*, p. 117.

54. For Correr's famous tragedy, satires, and hymn to Pope Martin V, see L. Casarsa, "Contributi per la biografia di Gregorio Correr," *Quaderni della Facoltà di Magistero di Trieste, Miscellanea I* (Udine, 1979), 29–88 at 35–39.

55. Song of Solomon 2:1 (Canticle of Canticles 2:1, Vulgate).

56. Psalm 121:1–2 (120:1–2, Vulgate).

57. Matthew 6:21; Luke 12:34.

58. John 12:26.

59. Mentioned earlier, see above, n. 8.

## *Selection 18*

1. On Francesco Barbaro, see G. Gualdo in *DBI* 6 (1964):101–3; and King, *Venetian Humanism in an Age of Patrician Dominance* pp. 323–25.

2. On Fabius' funeral oration, see Plutarch, *Life of Fabius*, 1.5 and 34.4. We find no similar incident regarding Julius Caesar who, in any case, did not have a son. It was a topos of antiquity that great men retain their composure in all circumstances.

3. Petrarch praises King Robert's composure on the death of his son in *Seniles* 10 (*Opera Omnia*, 3 vols. [Basel, 1554, repr. Ridgewood, N.J., 1965]), 2.166–73. See G. W. McClure, *Sorrow and Consolation in Italian Humanism* (Princeton, 1990), 41, 200 n. 64.

4. Boccaccio, *Concerning Famous Women*, chap. 79, mentions Julia's death but not Caesar's reaction (his source was Valerius Maximus). Others do the same: Plutarch *Life of Caesar* 23. 4; Suetonius, 1. 25–26; Dio Cassius, 39. 64.

5. Francesco Foscari and Federico Contarini were both prominent Venetian statesmen—the former Doge from 1423 until 1457—and contemporaries of Barbaro. Their stoicism in face of their children's death must have been famous in their day.

6. See Jerome, # 118 (PL 22:960–66; NPNF, ser. 2, 6:222–23).

7. Cf. Socrates in Plato's *Apology* (41) who remarks that no harm can come to a good man, either in this life or after death.

8. Lorenzo Giustiniani, Bishop of Castello (1433), later Patriarch (1451) and Saint (1524), was from a patrician family in Venice. On him, see especially *San Lorenzo Giustiniani, Protopatriarca di Venezia nel V centenario di morte, 1456–1956* (Venice, 1959). His brothers, Marco and Leonardo, were important statesmen of Barbaro's generation, and Leonardo was also a famous humanist and poet. For material on Leonardo and the Giustiniani family, see the bibliography of secondary sources in Patricia H. Labalme, *Bernardo Giustiniani: A Venetian of the Quattrocento*, Uomini e Dottrine, vol. 13 (Rome, 1969), pp. 338–44.

9. On Ermolao Barbaro the Elder, Francesco's nephew and thus in fact Costanza's cousin, and a humanist in the grand family tradition, see E. Bigi in *DBI* 6 (1964):95–96; and King, *Venetian Humanism in an Age of Patrician Dominance*, pp. 320–22.

10. See Job 42.

11. See Genesis 22.

12. See Genesis 37–48.

13. There is no such incident recorded in Ezekiel. But see Ezekiel 33:9. The statement fits more closely the prophet Elijah who is several times sent into hiding by God to save his life. See I Kings 17–19 (III Kings 17–19, Vulgate).

14. See Mark 8.31–33; Matthew 16:21–23.

15. See Acts 9:3–9; 22:6–16.

16. See Romans 11:34.

17. See Hosea 14:10.

18. See Romans 12:2: "Do not be conformed to this world but be transformed by the renewal of your mind, that you may prove what is the will of God, what is good and acceptable and perfect;" see also I John 2:15–17.

19. Virgil *Aeneid* 6. 625.

20. See Matthew 19:12.


## *Selection 19*

1. On Lauro Quirini, see *Lauro Quirini umanista: studi e testi*, ed. V. Branca et al., Civiltà veneziana, saggi 23 (Florence, 1977); and King, *Venetian Humanism in an Age of Patrician Dominance*, 419–21.

2. The Aristotelian tradition at Padua, to which Quirini's letter is a testimony, has been much studied in the last two decades. For brief introductions, see especially J. H. Randall, Jr., *The School of Padua and the Emergence of Modern Science* (Padua, 1961); P. O. Kristeller, *La tradizione aristotelica nel Rinascimento* (Padua, 1962); and A. Poppi, *Introduzione all'aristotelismo padovano* (Padua, 1970).

3. Cf. Cicero *Ad Fam.* 5. 12. 1.

4. This could be the Aristotelian philosophy, as is made clear later in the letter.

5. See above, selection 14, n. 4.

6. See above, selection 9, n. 5.

7. See above, selection 14, n. 12.

8. See above, selection 14, n. 14.

9. Amesia Sentia pleaded her own cause before her Roman judges and was so eloquent that she was acquitted by a unanimous vote. She was said to carry the soul of a man in the body of a woman and so was named Androgyne. See Valerius Maximus, 8. 6. 1.

10. See above, selection 14, n. 17.

11. See above, selection 9, n. 6.

12. Hypatia (c. 375–415) was a Neoplatonist philosopher of Alexandria who wrote on philosophy and mathematics (her father Theon had been a mathematician). Synesius, Bishop of Ptolemais, was one of her pupils. Synesius addressed seven letters to Hypatia; several are addressed to her by name, several others to the Philosopher, where clearly she is meant. He venerated her, as his letters both to her and to others clearly show. Since he is the only philosopher known to us influenced by her, it is unfortunate that his letters reveal nothing of her thought. We can infer that she was a Platonist, as was Synesius (letter #s 10, 15, 16, 33, 81 [80], 124, 154 [153]): PG 66:1348, 1352, 1362, 1452–54, 1504, 1554–58; *The Letters of Synesius of Cyrene*, trans. A. Fitzgerald [Oxford, 1926], 95–96, 99–100, 108, 174, 214, 250–54; where the numbering differs the bracketed numbers are those in Migne). Hypatia was killed by a Christian mob on the suspicion that she had set the pagan prefect of Alexandria against the Christians. Charles Kingsley made her life the basis of a novel, *Hypatia* (1853).

13. Cicero *De off* 1. 18. 61.

14. I.e., find difficulties where there are none. See Plautus, *Menaechmi*, Act 2,

scene 1, line 22; and Terence, *Andria*, Act 5, scene 4, line 38.

15. Publilius Syrus in Aulus Gellius, *Noctes Atticae*, 17. 14. 4.

16. Antistius Labeo was a renowned legal authority contemporary with the Emperor Augustus. He founded one of the two principal schools of Roman jurisprudence, that which believed in making innovations in the law as reason and philosophy require. Many of his opinions are embodied in the *Corpus Iuris Civilis*, compiled under the Emperor Justinian in the sixth century, used by Quirini, and still used today for the study of Roman law.

17. See *Metaphysics*, 1. 5. 986b17–31.

18. Boethius (c. 480–c.524) was both a philosopher and a statesman. He became the friend and adviser of Theodoric. He was subsequently accused of treason and executed. While in prison awaiting execution, he wrote his most famous work, *The Consolation of Philosophy*, which describes how the soul attains a vision of God through philosophy. He was also a classical scholar of major importance. See the following note.

19. For Boethius' works on the dialectical art, see *Introductio ad Syllogismos categoris* (PL 64:761–94); *De Syllogismo categorico libri duo* (PL 64:793–832); *De Syllogismo hypothetico libri duo* (PL 64:831–76); *Liber de divisione* (PL 64:875–92); *Liber de diffinitione* (PL 64:891–910). For his commentary on Aristotle's *Categories*, see PL 64:159–294. And for his work on Aristotle's *On Interpretation*, see PL 64:293–392.

20. Reference here is doubtless to the works Aristotle classified as practical, that is, those related to knowledge as a guide to conduct. This consisted of two parts: ethics and politics. See above, selection 4, n. 4.

21. What follows to the end of this paragraph is a description of the disciplines Aristotle classified as theoretical, that is, having to do with knowledge for its own sake: mathematics, physics, and metaphysics. See *Metaphysics* 6. 1.

22. Averroes (1126–98) came from the Spanish Moslem community in Cordova. He wrote a number of commentaries on Aristotle for which he was famous during the Middle Ages. Thomas Aquinas refers to him as the Commentator in his *Summa Theologica*, just as Thomas refers to Aristotle as the Philosopher. Quirini follows these designations in this passage.

23. Thomas Aquinas (1225–74) was a Dominican theologian, author of the *Summa contra gentiles* and *Summa Theologica*, the latter the principal work during the Middle Ages synthesizing Aristotelian philosophy with Christian faith. His work has since become a standard of theology in the Roman Catholic Church.

24. Avicenna (980–1037) was an Arabian Moslem philosopher, an early Aristotelian whose work influenced the Latin West. He was the author of some one hundred works, a number of which were translated into Latin. Al Ghazali (1058–1111) was a Moslem theologian from Iran. His inclination was mystical. However, in the Latin West he was known principally through a truncated translation of *The Intentions of Philosophers*, which made it appear as if he were a philosopher, whereas his intention was to be a critic of philosophy.

24a. Leonardo Bruni (1370–1444) was the first humanist to translate some of the texts of Aristotle. But it was only later in the quattrocento (after Quirini wrote this letter) that humanist translations of Aristotle were completed. The sentiments Quirini expresses here were widely shared by the humanists. Bruni opens his preface to the first humanist translation of Aristotle's *Ethics* (1416) with the comment: "I recently undertook to do into Latin Aristotle's *Ethics*, not because it had never been translated, but because it had been translated, as it would seem from the manner of it, rather by barbarians than by Latins." And in the preface to his translation of the *Politics* (1434) he writes: "My motive for translating and interpreting it has been the same as that which induced me eighteen years ago to translate the *Ethics*. For when I saw that those books of Aristotle, which in Greek are written in such an elegant style, had been reduced by the crime of a bad translator to something ridiculously absurd, and had many errors especially in matters of the greatest importance, I undertook the labor of a new translation, in the hope that this might be of use to people in this part of the world." *The Humanism of Leonardo Bruni: Selected Texts*, trans. and introd. G. Griffiths, J. Hankins, and D. Thompson (Binghamton, 1987), 213, 163.

25. See Cicero *De oratore* 2. 9. 36.

26. All the allusions here are to the life of the intellect. Apollo is the god of light and also of the mind. Mercury (the Greek god Hermes) was often represented in the Middle Ages as a scholar, and in the Renaissance was highly venerated as a symbol of aspiring intellect, the mediator between the human mind and divine wisdom. The Muses are nine female divinities, each of whom presides over one of the arts and sciences. Thus Isotta is being exalted as akin to the gods in intellect.

27. I.e., "I promise you sincerely, firmly." See Velleius, 2. 23. 4.

28. There is a play on the words Lauro (the author's name) and laurel (the tree). To say that the laurel always remains green, i.e., never dies, signifies that Lauro's affection for Isotta will never change. The laurel wreath was also the reward given to poets.

29. Hippolytus' step-mother, Phaedra, conceived a passion for him which he repulsed. She hanged herself but left a note to her husband Theseus (father of Hippolytus) implicating Hippolytus. Theseus banished him and he was killed when his horses, frightened by Poseidon (acting on Theseus' wish) dragged him to death. Theseus later learned the truth. See Euripides, *Hippolytus* and Seneca, *Phaedra*.

30. Cicero, *On Duties*, 2.2.5–6. See also *Tusculan Disputations*, 1.26.64–65. The sentiment that Quirini expresses as his own in the following sentence is also expressed by Cicero in the second of the passages cited.

31. Cf. Cicero, *Ad. Fam.* 10.12.2.

## Selection 20

1. Ellipsis in text.

2. See above, selection 11, n. 8. The story referred to here is told in Plutarch's *Life of Lycurgus* 9. 1–2.

3. The source for this saying, which may not be a quotation, may be Diogenes Laertius. The sentiment expressed is certainly in Diogenes. For example: "They have the sweetest enjoyment of luxury who stand least in need of it." (Diogenes Laertius, *Epicurus*, 10.130; *Diogenes Laertius*, trans. R. D. Hicks [Cambridge, MA, 1958], 2.655) "Nature's wealth at once has its bounds and is easy to procure, but

the wealth of vain fancies recedes to an infinite distance." And: "Fortune but seldom interferes with the wise man; his greatest and highest interests have been, are, and will be, directed by reason throughout the course of his life." (Ibid., 10.144; tr. 2.669).

4. We have omitted one sentence here which is broken and not fully intelligible.

5. See Romans 12:1.

6. See Acts 7:22.

7. See Daniel 1:17–20.

8. We are unable to locate the name Geno.

9. Ellipses here and in the remainder of this paragraph are in the text.

10. See Virgil *Aeneid* 6. 782.

11. See John 3:8.

12. Two half-sentences which make no sense as they stand have been omitted here.

13. See above, selection 14, n. 16 and 18.

14. See above, selection 14, n. 12.

15. In the biblical account Solomon does not praise the Queen of Sheba; it is rather the queen who praises him. See above, selection 14, n. 3. Cicero (106–43) and Virgil (70–19) were, respectively, the greatest prose writer and the greatest poet of classical Rome. Augustine (354–430) and Jerome (342–420) were the greatest theologians of the Latin West. Thus Isotta is said to prefer the best of both the classical pagan and the Christian traditions.

16. Perhaps a local person of some renown. She is unknown to us.

17. Ellipsis in text.

18. See Virgil *Aeneid* 1. 379.

19. Giuliano Cesarini (1398–1444) received a doctorate of laws from Bologna and then taught there; among his students was Nicholas of Cusa. Later, as an ecclesiastic, he was sent on a number of diplomatic missions and was widely regarded for his persuasive powers and his refusal to accept favors from anyone. He became a cardinal in 1430. In 1431 he attended the Council of Basel where he adopted the conciliar point of view, even leading the council in that direction. But when the pope shifted the council to Italy, he went there, subsequently becoming a spokesman for the pope. He died leading an army against the Hussites in 1444. Vespasanio da Bisticci included him in his lives of illustrious men of the fifteenth century (see *Renaissance Princes, Popes and Prelates*, trans. W. George and E. Waters, intro. M. P. Gilmore (New York, 1963), pp. 125–32). For a modern critical biography see Joseph Gill, S. J., *Personalities of the Council of Florence and Other Essays* (New York, 1964), pp. 95–103.

20. Ellipsis in text.

## Selection 21

1. Felix Tadinus was addressed by Cereta as a philosopher. He is otherwise unknown to us. She wrote three letters to him, one of which has existed until recently only in manuscript form. It has now been published in Rabil, *Laura Cereta*, part 3, no. 7. The letter referred to here by Fra Tommaso is in Tomasini,

*Laurae Ceretae epistolae*, pp. 59–60. For a summary of the letter see Rabil, part 2, no. 57.

2. Cereta wrote only one letter to Sigismundus de Buccis, a lawyer in Brescia, but otherwise unknown to us. The letter is published in Tomasini, *Laurae Ceretae epistolae*, pp. 12–17 and summarized in Rabil, *Laura Cereta*, part 2, no. 29.

3. See *Odyssey* 2. 104–5.

4. The reference to the Amazon pleasing Theseus refers to Theseus' courtship of the Amazon Hippolyta (Antiope). See Plutarch *Life of Theseus* p. 26ff. We can find no reference to a Babylonian Lucretia and her relation to Frederick Augustus.

5. Two letters fit this description. The first is to Ludovico Cendrata, a well-known humanist from Verona, student and relative of Guarino of Verona and correspondent of Isotta Nogarola. Cereta wrote only one letter to him (and he did not write to her, as far as we know). It is published in Tomasini, *Laurae Ceretae epistolae*, pp. 206–14 and summarized in Rabil, *Laura Cereta*, part 2, no. 35. The second is to Clementine Longulus, a grammarian, but otherwise unknown to us. It is published in Tomasini, pp. 81–83 and summarized in Rabil, part 2, no. 66.

6. This has been published for the first time in Rabil, *Laura Cereta*, part 3, no. 1 and summarized in the same source, part 2, no. 1.

7. See this anthology, selection 13.

8. There are several letters which contain such descriptions, for Cereta was an accomplished astrologer. See Tomasini, *Laurae Ceretae epistolae*, pp. 71, 109–10, 125–29; and for summaries, Rabil, *Laura Cereta*, part 2, nos. 37, 36, and 24 respectively.

9. See Tomasini, *Laurae Ceretae epistolae*, pp. 133–37 and Rabil, *Laura Cereta*, part 2, no. 21.

10. The letter here referred to was addressed to Cassandra Fedele, whom Cereta urged to reply to her, though Cassandra never did. It is published in Tomasini, *Laurae Ceretae epistolae*, pp. 75–80 and summarized in Rabil, *Laura Cereta*, part 2, no. 55.

11. See Luke 8:2; Mark 15:40; 16:1ff.; Matthew 28:9; John 20:11ff.

12. Acts 9:36–43.

13. We can find no reference to a Drusiana in biblical or patristic Christian literature.

14. Eustochium (370–419) was the daughter of Paula. Both women left Rome with Jerome and traveled to Bethlehem, where they established four monasteries. Paula, and after her death in 404, Eustochium, governed these. Jerome addressed to Paula, among others, letter 39 (PL 22:465–73; NPNF, ser. 2, 6:49–54) and to Eustochium his famous letter 22 (see above, selection 17, note 8), 31 (PL 22:445–46; NPNF, ser. 2, 6:45), and 108 (PL 22:878–906; NPNF, ser. 2, 6:195–212). Letter 46 (PL 22:483–92; NPNF, ser. 2, 6:60–65) is probably from Paula and Eustochium to Jerome.

15. Scholastica (480–543) was the sister of Benedict of Nursia. She is mentioned in the Dialogues (2. 33ff.) of Gregory the Great, the only source of our knowledge of her. She established a convent at Plombariola, a few miles from Monte Cassino. She met with her brother annually to discuss spiritual matters.

16. These are all famous Christian leaders of the fourth and fifth centuries. Macharius was a Christian apologist of the fourth or fifth century, Bishop of

Magnesia. Antony (251–356) was a famous ascetic, one of the founders of monasticism. Ambrose, Augustine, Jerome, and Gregory we have encountered before. See above, selection 17, n. 48.

## Selection 22

1. Lucan (39–65), author of the *Pharsalia*, was the nephew of Seneca (4 B.C.E.–65 C.E.), the Stoic philosopher and close political adviser of Nero. They belonged to the so-called "Silver Age" of Latin literature, somewhat less exalted than the "Golden Age" of Augustus. The implication here, of course, is that Fra Tommaso did not learn his style (as Cereta did) from the purest sources of classical Latin, but from derivative sources. In a way, he is saying that he is not as learned as Cereta, which he says explicitly in another of his letters—one indication that he was not her teacher.

## Selection 23

1. On Poliziano, see E. Bigi in *DBI* 2 (1960):691–702, and sources cited.

2. The text appears also in Poliziano's correspondence, most conveniently in Poliziano's *Opera Omnia* vol. 1, ed. Aldo Maier, Monumenta politica philosophica humanistica rariora, ser. 1, no. 16 (Turin, 1971), which is a reprint of the *Epistolarum libri duodecim* (Basel, 1553), pp. 38–39.

3. Virgil *Aeneid* 11. 508–9.

4. On the Muses, see Hesiod, *Theogony*, pp. 53–104 and *passim*. On the Sibylline oracles, see Boccaccio, *Concerning Famous Women*, chaps. 19 and 24.

5. The text reads *Pythias*. The Pythia was the medium (who was female) at the shrine of Apollo at Delphi.

6. Diogenes Laertius, 8.42, refers to Theano, the wife of Pythagoras and his daughter Damo. The latter, according to Diogenes, was put in charge of Pythagoras' memoirs after his death.

7. Diotima was the legendary priestess of Mantinea and teacher of Socrates into whose mouth Plato placed his metaphysic of love in the *Symposium*, 201F–212A.

8. See above, selection 9, n. 5.

9. In the list of names that follows in this sentence, all but the last are mentioned in a fragment, *The Greek Anthology*, 9:26.

10. Telesilla was an Argive poetess of the fifth century B.C.E., famous for arming the women of Argos after its defeat by Cleomenes (see Pausanias, 2.20.8–10). Nine fragments of her work survive and seem to come from hymns, especially to Apollo and Artemis, with whom six are concerned. She seems to have written mainly for women. The Telesilleion, a Greek metre, is named after her. See *The Oxford Classical Dictionary*, p. 882.

11. Corinna was a lyric poetess of Tanagra in Boeotia, an older contemporary of Pindar (518–438), over whom she won a victory at Thebes with one of her lyric poems (see Pausanias, 9.22.3). She wrote for a circle of women on Boeotian subjects. Substantial fragments of two of her poems remain. See *The Oxford Classical Dictionary*, p. 235.

12. On Sappho, see above, selection 14, n. 12.

13. Anyte (fl. 290 B.C.E.) was an Arcadian poetess, known from twenty Doric epigrams. Twelve are mock-epitaphs on pet animals; most of the others are nature-lyrics. See *The Greek Anthology*, 9.144, 313, 314, 745; 16.228, 231, 291; and *The Oxford Classical Dictionary*, p. 65.

14. Erinna was a poetess of the Dorian island of Telos who lived at the end of the fourth century B.C.E. She was famous for her *Distaff*, a poem in 300 hexameters in memory of her friend Baucis. She died when she was only nineteen. For extant fragments of her poems, see *The Greek Anthology*, 6:352; 7:710, 712; for statements about her, see ibid., 7:11–12, 713, 9:190.

15. Praxilla (fl. 451 B.C.E.) was a poetess of Sicyon who wrote dithyrambs, drinking songs, and hymns, including one to Adonis. See *The Oxford Classical Dictionary*, p. 727. She is mentioned in *The Greek Anthology*, 3.26.

16. Cleobulina was the mother of Thales, though nothing else about her is known. See Diogenes Laertius, 1. 22.

17. Laelia, daughter of Laelius, was the mother-in-law of L. Crassius. For her learning see Cicero *Brutus* 58. 211.

18. See Boccaccio, *Concerning Famous Women*, chap. 82.

19. See above, selection 9, n. 6.

20. The oration referred to is probably the one in this anthology, selection 11.

21. Cf. Virgil *Aeneid* 1. 493. Cassandra is being likened to Penthesilea, leader of the Amazon warriors. On Penthesilea see Boccaccio, *Concerning Famous Women*, chap. 30.

22. "Neither Thracian . . . side," see Virgil *Eclogues* 4. 55–57.

23. Pico della Mirandola (1463–1494) was a contemporary of Poliziano's in Florence, learned in Hebrew as well as in Greek and Latin, who aspired to universal knowledge and was recognized in his own lifetime as one of the intellectual lights of his age. On him, see P. O. Kristeller, "Pico della Mirandola, Count Giovanni," *Encyclopedia of Philosophy* 6 (1967), 307–11.

## Selection 24

1. See E. Safarik in *DBI* (1974), 17:317–18.

2. There is perhaps an allusion here to her namesake, Cassandra, daughter of Priam, king of Troy, a prophetess. See Aeschylus, *Agamemnon*, 1203ff.; Virgil *Aeneid* 2. 246–47.

3. The letter referred to was published by Cavazzana with the letter here translated: *L'Ateneo Veneto* (1906), pp. 384–86. Fra Girolamo Monopolitano was a teacher of theology belonging to the Dominican Order.

4. See Cicero, *On Old Age*, 49.

5. The reference is to Pope Gregory I, 590–604.

6. In her letter to Monopolitano (see above, n. 3) Fedele cites the opinion of St. Gregory that it is difficult to be saved and that few attain salvation, an opinion which seems to contradict the idea of divine mercy. Conceived in sin, it appears that we are all condemned. But God has become visible and taken on flesh in Christ, who has atoned for the sins of one and all who accept him. And who

would not accept him under such circumstances? Thus it seems that all should be saved. What are we, then, to make of the opinion of Gregory?

7. Matthew 18:22.
8. Matthew 16:18.
9. Mark 14:72; Matthew 26:75; Luke 22:62.
10. Luke 23:32, 39–43.

# Bibliography

## Primary Sources

Alberti, Leon Battista. *I libri della famiglia* in *Opera volgari*. Vol. 1. Edited by C. Grayson. Bari, 1960, pp. 1–341; Translated by R. N. Watkins. *The Family in Renaissance Florence*. Columbia, SC, 1969.

Barbaro, Francesco. *De re uxoria*. Edited by A. Gnesotto. *Atti e Memorie della Regia Accademia di scienze lettere ed arti di Padova*, n.s., 32 (1915): 6–105; preface and book 2 translated by B. G. Kohl, "On Wifely Duties." In *The Earthly Republic: Italian Humanists on Government and Society*. Edited by Kohl and R. G. Witt. Philadelphia, 1978, pp. 179–228.

Barbaro, Francesco. *Francisci Barbari et aliorum ad ipsum epistolae*. Edited by A. M. Querini. Brescia, 1743, pp. 127–33 (our selection 18).

Birgitta of Sweden, Saint. *The Revelations of Saint Birgitta*. Edited by W. P. Cumming from the fifteenth-century manuscript in the Garrett Collection in the Library of Princeton University. Early English Text Society, by Humphrey Milford. London, 1929.

Boccaccio, Giovanni. *De mulieribus claris*. Edited by V. Zaccaria. In *Tutte le opere di Giovanni Boccaccio*. Vol. 10. Edited by V. Branca. Verona, 2nd ed., 1970, Latin and Italian; Translated by G. A. Guarino. *Concerning Famous Women*. New Brunswick, NJ, 1963.

Branca, V., et al. *Lauro Quirini umanista: Studi e testi*. Civiltà veneziana, saggi 23. Florence, 1977.

Brucker, G., ed. *Two Memoirs of Renaissance Florence: The Diaries of Buonaccorso Pitti and Gregorio Dati*. Translated by J. Martines. New York, 1967.

———, ed. *The Society of Renaissance Florence: A Documentary Study*. New York, 1971.

Bruni, Leonardo. "De studiis et literis." Translated by W. H. Woodward. *Vittorino da Feltre and Other Humanist Educators*. Cambridge, 1897; reprinted with an introduction by E. F. Rice, Jr., New York, 1963, pp. 119–33. Also translated in Griffiths, et al., *The Humanism of Leonardo Bruni* (q.v.), pp. 140–51 (to Battista da Montefeltro Malatesta).

Castiglione, Baldesar. *The Book of the Courtier*. Translated by C. S. Singleton. Garden City, NY, 1959. Also translated by G. Bull. New York, 1967.

Catherine of Siena. *The Letters of Catherine of Siena, Vol. 1: Letters 1–88.* Edited by S. Noffke. Binghamton, NY, 1988.

Cavazzani, C. "Cassandra Fedele: Erudita Veneziana del Rinascimento." *L'Ateneo Veneto* 29 (1906): appendix 9, pp. 386–87 (our selection 24).

Cereta, Laura. *Laurae Ceretae Epistolae.* Edited by J. F. Tomasini. Padua, 1640, pp. 66–70, 187–95, 122–25 (our selections 13, 14, 15, respectively).

Contarini, G. B. "Corrarii epistola ad Caeciliam virginem de fugiendo saeculo." *Anecdota Veneta.* Venice, 1757, pp. 33–44 (our selection 17).

Conti Odorisio, G., ed. *Donna e società nel Seicento.* Biblioteca di cultura, 167. Rome, 1979, Part 2 (texts of Lucrezia Marinelli, Moderata Fonte, and Arcangela Tarabotti).

Corvisieri, C. *Notabilia temporum di Angelo de Tummulillis da Sant'Elia.* Fonti per la storia d'Italia, vol. 7. Livorno, 1890, pp. 231–33 (our selection 6).

Costa-Zalessow, N., ed. *Scrittrici italiane dal XVIII al XX secolo: Testi e critica.* L'interprete, 32. Ravenna, 1982.

Dronke, P. *Women Writers of the Middle Ages: A Critical Study of Texts from Perpetua (+203) to Marguerite Porete (+1310).* Cambridge, 1984.

Durand, U., and E. Martène, eds. *Veterum scriptorum et monumentorum historicorum, dogmaticorum, moralium, amplissima collectio.* Vol. 3. Paris, 1724, cols. 829–42 (alternative text to our selection 17).

Erasmus, Desiderius. *The Colloquies of Erasmus.* Translated by C. R. Thompson. Chicago, 1965.

———. *Opus epistolarum Des. Erasmi Roterodami.* Edited by P. S. Allen, et al., 12 vols. Oxford, 1906–58. Translated by R. A. B. Mynors and D. F. S. Thomson. *The Correspondence of Erasmus.* Collected Works of Erasmus. Vols. 1–9 to date. Toronto, 1974–.

Fattori, A., and B. Feliciangeli. "Lettere inedite di Battista da Montefeltro." *Rendiconti della Regia Accademia dei Lincei, Classe di scienze morali, storiche e filologiche,* ser. 5, 26 (1917): 196–215.

Fedele, Cassandra. *Cassandrae Fidelis Venetae: Epistolae et orationes.* Edited by J. F. Tomasini. Padua, 1636, pp. 207–10, 193–201, 201–7, 163–64, 164 (our selections 7, 11, 12, 16, respectively).

Foresti, Giacomo Filippo Bergomensis. *De memorabilibus et claris mulieribus, aliquot diversorum scriptorum opera.* Paris, 1521.

Griffiths, G., J. Hankins, and D. Thompson, eds. *The Humanism of Leonardo Bruni: Selected Texts.* Medieval & Renaissance Texts & Studies, 46; RSA Renaissance Texts Series, 10. Binghamton, NY, 1987.

Guarino of Verona. *Epistolario di Guarino Veronese.* Edited by R. Sabbadini, 3 vols. Venice, 1915–19.

Kempe, Margery. *The Book of Margery Kempe, 1436.* Translated by W. Butler-Bowden. London, 1936.

Kohl, B. G., and R. G. Witt, eds. *The Earthly Republic: Italian Humanists on Government and Society.* Philadelphia, 1978.

Kors, A. C., and E. Peters, eds. *Witchcraft in Europe, 1100–1700: A Documentary History.* Philadelphia, 1972.

Krämer (Institoris), Heinrich, and Jacob Sprenger. *Malleus Maleficarum.* Edited and translated by M. Summers. London, 1928; reprint, New York, 1971.

Lamius, J. *Catalogus codicum manuscriptorum qui in Bibliotheca Riccardiana Florentiae adservantur....* Livorno, 1756, pp. 145–50 (our selections 3, 4, and 8).

Machiavelli, Niccolò. *The Prince.* Edited by T. G. Bergin. New York, 1947.

Medin, A. "Maddalena degli Scrovegni e le discordie tra i Carraresi e gli Scrovegni." *Atti e Memorie della Regia Accademia di scienze, lettere ed arti in Padova* 12 (1896): 260–72 (our selection 1).

Meersseman, G. G. "La raccolta dell'umanista fiammingo Giovanni de Veris 'De arte epistolandi'." *Italia medioevale e umanistica* 15 (1972): 250–51 (our selection 5).

Mittarelli, G. B. *Bibliotheca codicum manuscriptorum monasterii Sancti Michaelis Venetiarum prope Murianum.* Venice, 1779, cols. 701–2 (our selection 2).

Morata, Olympia. *Olympiae Fulviae Moratae foeminae doctissimae ac plane divinae orationes, dialogi, epistolae, carmina, tam Latina quam Graeca.* Edited by Celio Secondo Curione. 3rd ed. Basel, 1570.

———. *Opere.* Edited by Lanfranco Caretti. *Deputazione provinciale ferrarese di storia patria, Atti e Memorie,* n.s., 11 (1954), Parts 1 (Epistolae) and 2 (Orationaes, dialogi et carmina).

Nogarola, Isotta. *Isotae Nogarolae Veronensis opera quae supersunt omnia.* Edited by E. Abel, 2 vols. Vienna and Budapest, 1886, 2:3–6, 187–216, 9–22, 39–51 (our selections 9, 10, 19, 20, respectively).

O'Faolain, J., and L. Martines, eds. *Not in God's Image: Women in History from the Greeks to the Victorians.* New York, 1973.

Petroff, E. A., ed. *Medieval Women's Visionary Literature.* New York, 1986.

Piccolomini, Enea Silvio. *Memoirs of a Renaissance Pope: The Commentaries of Pius II.* Translated by F. A. Gragg. Edited by L. C. Gabel. Abr. Ed. New York, 1962.

de Pizan, Christine. *The Book of the City of Ladies.* Translated by E. J. Richards. New York, 1982.

Poliziano, Angelo. *Opera omnia.* Vol. 1. Edited by A. Maïer. Monumenta politica philosophica humanistica rariora, Ser. 1, No. 16. Turin, 1971 (alternative text to our selection 23).

Rabil, A. Jr. *Laura Cereta: Quattrocento Humanist*. Binghamton, 1981, Part 3. Contains one oration and eleven letters not in the Tomasini edition (q.v.) of her works (numbers 9 and 10, our selections 21 and 22).

Roncini, G., ed. *Ermolao Barbaro il vecchio, orationes contra poetas, epistolae*. Facoltà di Magistero dell'Università di Padova, vol. 14. Florence, 1972.

Simonsfeld, H. "Zur Geschichte der Cassandra Fedele." *Studien zur Literaturgeschichte, Michael Bernays gewidmet von Schülern und Freunden*. Hamburg and Leipzig, 1893, pp. 101–8.

Strozzi, Alessandra de'Macinghi. *Lettere di una gentildonna fiorentina del secolo XV*. Edited by C. Guasti. Florence, 1877.

Teresa of Avila, Saint. *The Life of Saint Teresa of Avila by Herself*. Translated by J. M. Cohen. New York, 1957.

Travitsky, B. S., ed. *The Paradise of Women: Writings by Englishwomen of the Renaissance*. Contributions in Women's Studies, 22. Westport, CT, 1981.

Varano, Costanza. *C. Varaneae Sfortiae Pisauri Principis orationes et epistolae*. In T. Bettinelli, ed. *Miscellanea di varie operette*, 7. Venice, 1743, pp. 295–330.

Warnke, F. J. *Three Women Poets, Renaissance and Baroque: Louise Labé, Gaspara Stampa, and Sor Juana Inés de la Cruz*. Lewisburg, PA, 1987.

Wilson, K. M., ed. *Medieval Women Writers*. Athens, GA, 1984.

———, ed. *Women Writers of the Renaissance and Reformation*. Athens, GA, 1987.

Woodward, W. H. *Vittorino da Feltre and Other Humanist Educators*. Cambridge, 1897; reprint, New York 1963, with foreword by E. F. Rice, Jr.

Zaccaria, V. "Una epistola metrica inedita di Antonio Loschi a Maddalena Scrovegni." *Bolletino del Museo Civico di Padova* 46 (1957–58): 153–68 (letter, 164–68).

Zonta, Giuseppe, ed. *Trattati del Cinquecento sulla donna*. Scrittori d'italia, 56. Bari, 1913.

## Secondary Sources

Agnelli, G. *Olimpia Morata*. Ferrara, 1892.

Anderson, B. S., and J. P. Zinsser. *A History of Their Own: Women in Europe from Prehistory to the Present*. 2 vols. New York, 1988.

Bainton, R. H. *Women of the Reformation in Germany and Italy.* Minneapolis, 1971.

———. *Women of the Reformation in France and England.* Minneapolis, 1973.

———. *Women of the Reformation from Spain to Scandinavia.* Minneapolis, 1977.

Barstow, A. *Joan of Arc: Heretic, Mystic, Shaman.* Lewiston, NY, 1986.

Bell, S. G. "Christine de Pizan (1364–1430): Humanism and the Problem of a Studious Woman." *Feminist Studies* 3 (1976): 172–84.

Bellonci, M. "Beatrice and Isabella d'Este." In *Renaissance Profiles,* edited by J. H. Plumb. New York, 1965, pp. 139–56.

Bigi, E. "Ambrogini, Angelo (Poliziano)." *Dizionario biografico degli italini* 2 (1960): 691–702.

———. "Barbaro, Ermolao the Elder." *Dizionario biografico degli italiani* 6 (1964): 95–96.

———. "Renée of France between Reform and Counter-Reform." *Archiv für Reformationsgeschichte* 63 (1972): 196–225.

Boccanera, G. *Biografica e scritti della B. Camilla Battista da Varano, clarissa di Camerino (1458–1524).* Rome, 1957.

Bonnet, Jules. *Vie d'Olympia Morata, épisode de la Renaissance et de la Réforme en Italie.* 3rd ed. Paris, 1856.

Boulting, W. *Women in Italy from the Introduction of the Chivalrous Service of Love to the Appearance of the Professional Actress.* New York, 1910.

Breisach, E. *Caterina Sforza: A Renaissance Virago.* Chicago, 1967.

Brown, J. C. *Immodest Acts: The Life of a Lesbian Nun in Renaissance Italy.* New York, 1986.

Bullough, V. L. *The Subordinate Sex: A History of Attitudes towards Women.* Urbana, IL, 1973.

Bynum, C. W. *Jesus as Mother: Studies in the Spirituality of the High Middle Ages.* Berkeley, 1982.

Cannon, M. A. *The Education of Women during the Renaissance.* Washington, DC, 1916.

Casarsa, L. "Contributi per la biografia di Gregorio Correr." *Quaderni della Facoltà di Magistero di Trieste, Miscellanea I.* Udine, 1979, pp. 29–88.

Cavazzana, C. "Cassandra Fedele: Erudita veneziana del Rinascimento." *Ateneo Veneto* 29 (1906), vol. 2: 73–91, 249–75, 361–97.

Chiappetti, P. M. *Vita di Costanza Varano.* Jesi, 1871.

Chojnacki, S. "Patrician Women in Early Renaissance Venice." *Studies in the Renaissance* 21 (1974): 176–203.

Conti Odorisio, G., ed. *Donna e società nel seicento.* Rome, 1979, Part 1 (on Lucrezia Marinelli, Moderata Fonte, and Arcangela Tarabotti).

Cosenza, M. *Biographical and Bibliographical Dictionary of the Italian Humanists and of the World of Classical Scholarship in Italy, 1300–1800*. 6 vols. 2nd edition. Boston, 1962.

Cotton, J. H. "Caldiera, Caterina." *Dizionario biografico degli italiani* 16 (1973): 626–28.

Cross, C. " 'Great Reasoners in Scripture': The Activities of Women Lollards 1380–1530." In *Medieval Women: Dedicated and Presented to Professor Rosalind M. T. Hill on the Occasion of Her Seventieth Birthday*, edited by D. Baker. Oxford, 1978, pp. 359–80.

Davis, N. Z. "Gender and Genre: Women as Historical Writers, 1400–1820." In Labalme, ed., *Beyond Their Sex* (q.v.), pp. 153–82.

De Maulde de la Clavière, A. M. R. *Les femmes de la Renaissance*. Paris, 1898.

Fahy, C. "Three Early Renaissance Treatises on Women." *Italian Studies* 11 (1956): 30–55.

Feliciangeli, B. "Notizie sulla vita e sugli scritti di Costanza Varano-Sforza (1426–1447)." *Giornale storico della letteratura italiana* 23 (1894): 1–75.

———. "Notizie della vita di Elisabetta Malatesta-Varano." *R. Dep. di Storia Patria per le Marche, Atti e Memorie*, n.s., 6 (1909–10): 171–216.

Felisatti, M. *Isabella d'Este, la primadonna del Rinascimento*. Milan, 1982.

Ferguson, M. W., M. Quilligan, and N. J. Vickers. *Rewriting the Renaissance: The Discourses of Sexual Difference in Early Modern Europe*. Chicago, 1986.

Ferrante, J. "The Education of Women in the Middle Ages in Theory, Fact, and Fantasy." In Labalme, ed., *Beyond Their Sex* (q.v.), 9–42.

Franceschini, G. "Battista Montefeltro Malatesta Signora di Pesaro." *Studia oliveriana* 6 (1958): 7–43.

Frati, L. *La donna italiana secondo i più recenti studi*. Turin, 1899, 2nd ed., 1928.

Garrard, M. D. *Artemisia Gentileschi: The Image of the Female Hero in Italian Baroque Art*. Princeton, 1989.

Gies, F. *Joan of Arc: The Legend and the Reality*. New York, 1981.

———, and J. Gies. *Women in the Middle Ages*. New York, 1978.

Gothein, P. "L'amicizia fra Ludovico Foscarini e l'umanista Isotta Nogarola." *Rinascita* 6 (1943): 394–413.

Grafton, A., and L. Jardine. *From Humanism to the Humanities: Education and the Liberal Arts in Fifteenth- and Sixteenth-Century Europe*. Cambridge, MA, 1985.

Grendler, P. *Schooling in Renaissance Italy: Literacy and Learning, 1300–1600*. Baltimore, 1989.

Gualdo, G. "Barbaro, Francesco." *Dizionario biografico degli italiani* 6 (1964): 101–3.

Gundersheimer, W. L. "Bartolommeo Goggio: A Feminist in Renaissance Ferrara." *Renaissance Quarterly* 23 (1980): 175–200.

———. "Women, Learning, and Power: Eleonora of Aragon and the Court of Ferrara." In Labalme, ed., *Beyond Their Sex* (q.v.), pp. 43–65.

Heiberg, J. L. "Beiträge zur Geschichte Georg Vallas und seiner Bibliothek." *Centralblatt für Bibliothekswesen* 13 (1896): 353–482.

Héritier, J. *Catherine de Medici.* Translated by C. Haldane. London, 1963.

Herlihy, D. "Did Women Have a Renaissance? A Reconsideration." *Medievalia et Humanistica*, n.s., 13 (1985): 1–22.

Hess, U. "Oratrix humilis: Die Frau als Briefpartnerin von Humanisten, am Beispiel der Caritas Pirckheimer." In F. J. Worstbrock, ed., *Der Brief im Zeitalter der Renaissance.* Deutsche Forschungsgemeinschaft: Kommision für Humanismus-forschung, 9 (Weinheim, 1983), pp. 173–203.

Jardine, L. "Isotta Nogarola: Women Humanists—Education for What?" *History of Education* 12 (1983): 231–44.

———. " 'O decus Italiae virgo,' or the Myth of the Learned Lady in the Renaissance." *Historical Journal* 28 (1985): 799–819.

Jones, A. R. "City Women and Their Audiences: Louise Labé and Veronica Franco." In Ferguson, et al., *Rewriting the Renaissance* (q.v.), pp. 299–316.

Jordan, C. *Renaissance Feminism: Literary Texts and Political Models.* Ithaca, NY, 1990.

———. "Boccaccio's In-Famous Women." In Levin and Watson, eds., *Ambiguous Realities* (q.v.), 25–47.

———. "Feminism and the Humanists: The Case of Sir Thomas Elyot's Defence of Good Women." In Ferguson, et al., *Rewriting the Renaissance* (q.v.), 242–58.

Kaufman, G. "Juan Luis Vives on the Education of Women." *Signs* 3 (1978): 891–96.

Kelly, J. *Women, History, and Theory: The Essays of Joan Kelly.* Chicago, 1984:
1. "The Social Relation of the Sexes: Methodological Implications of Women's History" (1–18).
2. "Did Women Have a Renaissance?" (19–50).
3. "The Doubled Vision of Feminist Theory" (51–64).
4. "Early Feminist Theory and the *Querelle des Femmes*" (65–109).
5. " Family and Society" (110–55).

———. "Notes on Women in the Renaissance." In *Conceptual Frameworks in Women's History.* Bronxville, 1976.

Kelso, R. *Doctrine for the Lady of the Renaissance.* Urbana, IL, 1956. Extensive bibliography, pp. 304–462.

Kieckhefer, R. *Unquiet Souls: Fourteenth-Century Saints and Their Religious Milieu.* Chicago, 1984.

King, M. L. *Venetian Humanism in an Age of Patrician Dominance.* Princeton, 1986.

———. *Women of the Renaissance.* Chicago, 1991.

———. "Book-Lined Cells: Women and Humanism in the Early Italian Renaissance." In Labalme, ed. *Beyond Their Sex* (q.v.), pp. 66–90. See nn. 91ff. for bibliographical references to primary and secondary sources.

———. "Goddess and Captive: Antonio Loschi's Poetic Tribute to Maddalena Scrovegni (1389), Study and Text." *Medievalia et Humanistica,* n.s., 10 (1980): 103–27.

———. "Personal, Domestic, and Republican Values in the Moral Philosophy of Giovanni Caldiera." *Renaissance Quarterly* 28 (1975): 535–74.

———. "The Religious Retreat of Isotta Nogarola (1418–1466): Sexism and Its Consequences in the Fifteenth Century." *Signs* 3 (1978): 807–22.

———. "Thwarted Ambitions: Six Learned Women of the Italian Renaissance." *Soundings* 59 (1976): 180–304. See bibliography, 300–304.

Kristeller, P. O. *Iter Italicum: A Finding List of Uncatalogued or Incompletely Catalogued Humanistic Manuscripts of the Renaissance in Italian and other Libraries.* 6 vols. London and Leiden, 1963–92.

———. *La tradizione aristotelica nel Rinascimento.* Padua, 1962.

———. "Learned Women of Early Modern Italy: Humanists and University Scholars." In Labalme, ed., *Beyond Their Sex* (q.v.), pp. 91–116. See nn. 106ff. for bibliographical references.

Labalme, P. H. *Bernardo Giustiniani: A Venetian of the Quattrocento.* Uomini e Dottrine, vol. 13. Rome, 1969.

———, ed. *Beyond Their Sex: Learned Women of the European Past.* New York, 1980.

———. "Venetian Women on Women: Three Early Modern Feminists." *Archivio Veneto,* ser. 5, 197 (1981): 81–109.

———. "Women's Roles in Early Modern Venice: An Exceptional Case." In Labalme, ed., *Beyond Their Sex* (q.v.), pp. 129–52.

Latz, D. *Saint Angela Merici and the Spiritual Currents of the Italian Renaissance.* Lille, France, 1986.

Lenzi, M. L. *Donne e madonne: L'educazione femminile nel primo Rinascimento italiano.* Turin, 1982.

Levin, C., and J. Watson, eds. *Ambiguous Realities: Women in the Middle Ages and Renaissance.* Detroit, 1987.

MacLean, I. *The Renaissance Notion of Women: A Study in the Fortunes of Scholasticism and Medical Science in European Intellectual Life.* Cambridge Monographs on the History of Medicine. Cambridge, 1980.

McClure, G. W. *Sorrow and Consolation in Italian Humanism.* Princeton, 1991.

Maschietto, F. L. *Elena Lucrezia Cornaro Piscopia (1646–1684), prima donna laureata nel mondo.* Contributi alla storia dell'Università di Padova, 10. Padua, 1978.

Masetti Zannini, G. L. *Motivi storici della educazione femminile: scienza, lavoro, giuochi, con appendici di documenti.* Naples, 1982.

Medin, A. "Maddalena degli Scrovegni e le discordie tra i Carraresi e gli Scrovegni." *Atti e Memorie della Regia Accademia di scienze, lettere, ed arti in Padova* 12 (1896): 243–59.

Migiel, M., and J. Schiesari. *Refiguring Woman: Perspectives on Gender and the Italian Renaissance.* Ithaca, NY, 1991.

Musatti, E. *La donna in Venezia.* Padua, 1891.

Pereira, M., ed. *Nè Eva n Maria: Condizione femminile e immagine della donna nel Medioevo, con una raccolta di testi.* Letture storiche, 20. Bologna, 1981.

Pesenti, G. "Alessandra Scala, una figurina della Rinascenza fiorentina." *Giornale storico della letteratura italiana* 85 (1925): 241–67.

Pitkin, H. F. *Fortune Is a Woman: Gender and Politics in the Thought of Niccolò Macchiavelli.* Berkeley, CA, 1984.

*Il Poliziano e il suo tempo.* Atti del 18 Convegno Internazionale di Studi sul Rinascimento. Florence, 1957.

Poppi, A. *Introduzione all'aristotelismo padovano.* Padua, 1970.

Portigliotti, G. *Some Fascinating Women of the Renaissance.* Translated by B. Miall. New York, 1929.

Preto, P. "Correr, Gregorio." *Dizionario biografico degli italiani* 29 (1983): 497–500.

Rabil, A. Jr. *Laura Cereta: Quattrocento Humanist.* Binghamton, NY, 1981. Part 1, a critical biography, cites all the literature. Part 2 summarizes all her works.

Randall, J. H. Jr. *The School of Padua and the Emergence of Modern Science.* Padua, 1961.

Richards, E. J. "Introduction." *The Book of the City of Ladies.* By Christine de Pizan. New York, 1982, xix–xlvi.

Rodocanachi, E. P. *La femme italienne, avant, pendant, et après la renaissance.* Paris, 1922.

Rose, M. B., ed. *Women in the Middle Ages and the Renaissance: Literary and Historical Perspectives.* Syracuse, NY, 1986.

Rosenthal, M. F. "Veronica Franco's *Terze Rime*: The Venetian Courtesan's Defense." *Renaissance Quarterly* 42 (1989): 227–57.

Safarik, E. "Campagnola, Girolamo." *Dizionario biografico degli italiani* 17 (1974): 317–18.

*San Lorenzo Giustiniani, Protopatriarca di Venezia nel V centenario di morte, 1456–1956.* Venice, 1959.

Schutte, A. J. "Irene di Spilimbergo: The Image of a Creative Woman in Late Renaissance Italy." *Renaissance Quarterly* 44 (1991): 42–61.

Segarizzi, A. "Niccolò Barbo patrizio veneziano del secolo XV e le accuse contro Isotta Nogarola." *Giornale storico della letterature italiana* 43 (1904): 39–54.

———. "Lauro Quirini, umanista veneziano del secolo XV." *Memorie della Regia Accademia delle scienze di Torino,* ser. 2, 54 (1904): 1–28.

Simonsfeld, H. "Zur Geschichte der Cassandra Fedele." *Studien zur Literaturgeschichte, Michael Bernays gewidmet von Schülern und Freunden.* Hamburg and Leipzig, 1893, pp. 97–100.

Southey, E. A. B. *Olympia Morata, Her Times, Life and Writings.* London, 1834.

Sowards, J. K. "Erasmus and the Education of Women." *Sixteenth Century Journal* 13 (1982): 77–90.

Stinger, C. L. *Humanism and the Church Fathers: Ambrogio Traversari (1386–1439) and Christian Antiquity in the Italian Renaissance.* Albany, 1977.

Stuard, S. M., ed. *Women in Medieval Society.* Philadelphia, 1976.

Vorländer, D. "Olympia Fulvia Morata, eine evangelische Humanistin in Schweinfurt." *Zeitschrift für bayerischen Kirchengeschichte* 39 (1970): 95–113.

Waithe, M. E. *A History of Women Philosophers. II: Renaissance and Enlightenment Women Philosophers: 500–1600.* The Hague, 2nd ed., 1989.

Warnicke, R. M. *Women of the English Renaissance and Reformation.* Contributions in Women's Studies, 38. Westport, CT, 1983.

Willard, C. C. *Christine de Pizan: Her Life and Works.* New York, 1984.

Woodward, W. H. *Studies in Education during the Age of the Renaissance, 1400–1600.* Cambridge, 1924; reprint, New York, 1965.

Zaccaria, V. "Una epistola metrica inedita di Antonio Loschi a Maddalena Scrovegni." *Bolletino del Museo Civico di Padova* 46 (1957–58): 153–68 (letter, 164–68).

# Index